One Passionate Heart

A Journey into Intimacy with God

One Passionate Heart

A Journey into Intimacy with God

Laurie Steen Killingsworth

Cover photo of Laurie at 18 months taken by her father, Marshall Steen

ISBN 1-932768-06-8

Laurie Steen Killingsworth
One Passionate Heart

10 9 8 7 6 5 4 3

Academx Publishing Services, Inc.
547 Country Ridge Circle
Bel Air, MD 21015
410.569.9884
www. academx.com

Table of Contents

With a grateful heart ...

When I think of whom has impacted my life the most to bring me to this place of writing, my Lord and Savior Jesus Christ stands clearly above all others. "Work out your own salvation with fear and trembling; for it is God who works in you both to will and to do for His good pleasure" (Philippians 2:12b-13).

To facilitate His work in my life, He chose to give me a wonderful partner and companion who has done more to love and encourage me through the past three decades than any other person on the planet. "Husbands, love your wives, just as Christ also loved the church and gave Himself for her" (Ephesians 5:25). Thank you, Tip, for being the "wind beneath my wings." I love you.

"I have no greater joy than to hear that my children walk in truth" (3 John 4). I can say a passionate amen to that. As I bring my children before my heavenly Father daily, my heart's cry is that "their passion would be single" and that they would walk in truth. Thank you, Trey, Jason, Joshua, Trinity, and Karis for allowing me to be "my kid's mom." Your mom loves you.

I was blessed by God to be born into a prayer heritage that has gone before me for generations. It is not a perfect family, but it is a praying family. "Since we are surrounded by so great a cloud of witnesses, let us lay aside every weight, and the sin which so easily ensnares us, and let us run with endurance the race that is set before us, looking unto Jesus, the author and finisher of our faith" (Hebrews 12:1).

As I look gratefully to that cloud of witnesses, I realize that throughout eternity I will be thanking those who have gone before me. As I still have my wonderful dad and mom here on earth who continue to pray for me daily, I extend my abiding love and gratitude to them, Marshall and Cora Steen, for their deep and lasting impact in my life during those first eighteen formative years and beyond.

Acknowledgements

To name all those who encouraged me and held me up in prayer would be impossible, but they know who they are, and more importantly, God knows who they are. I humbly thank you.

I extend heartfelt thanks to my second-born son, Jason Andrew, who spent many hours lovingly editing this manuscript for me. God knew before the foundations of the world that he would graduate from the University of Florida with a major in English, and be able to serve his mom in such a valuable way. As I began to teach him how to read and write as a four-year old in our home in Dublin, Ireland, I had no idea that he would one day help to edit my first book.

I am grateful for Marge Buschbom, my dear friend and disciple, who spent many hours as a loving servant, editing and giving valuable advice. I also extend thanks to Kathy Ide in Brea, California. Even though I have never met her personally, computers have kept us in touch and she has been an extremely valuable advisor and editor as she walked me through the "learning curve" of this project.

Foreword

My desire and dream is that God would raise up people of power, purity, and prayer in every corner of our nation and beyond to walk intimately with their Bridegroom and to live out His plan for their lives. Since February 1995, God has been doing just that through Passionate Hearts (a conference ministry for women) and through many other avenues available to those who desire to be fully ready when their Bridegroom comes to take them to the wedding feast.

It is no mistake that you have picked up this book. It was God who brought you to this point in your life, and it is He who wants to walk with you from the gate of the Tabernacle all the way into the Holy of Holies. If we cannot live in power and victory in our own lives, how can we expect to help others to walk in freedom? It is a process, not a destination, and we are on this journey together.

My prayer is that you will read with an expectant and prayerful heart and with the readiness to listen to the voice of God. As He draws you into His awesome presence, ask Him to make you a "fire seed" for spiritual awakening and revival in your home, neighborhood, church, workplace, community, and nation until He returns.

Here we go!

Laurie

Prologue
I Miss Passion in My Life!

The dam finally broke. Standing by my bedroom door with my head resting against the wall, I cried aloud to the Lord, "I miss *passion* in my life! I have no passion for You, Lord, for my ministry, for my husband, for my friends, for the lost. *Please help me*!"

At that time, I had no idea God would bring me through three of the most difficult years of my life before restoring the passion I had prayed for. Nor did I see the vision He had for developing the Passionate Hearts conference ministry for women, which turned out to be another unexpected answer to my cry. But women of great passion almost always come through great pain. The most precious of God's jewels are crystallized tears. Some of the pain I endured during those three years was self-inflicted. But God allows *all* of our pain for a purpose.

The apostle Paul's driving passion was to be pleasing to God, and he didn't let obstacles —either recurring physical problems or relational issues — keep him from pursuing that goal.

Paul has always been both a challenge and an encouragement to me. Even though those dearest to him in Corinth nearly drove him to distraction at times (a couple of his most searing letters to them weren't even included in the Bible), he never wrote them off. He would not discount the good in them, despite the fact that their bad behavior deeply hurt him. He kept them in his heart regardless of whether or not they opened their hearts to him. He had "birthed them in Christ" and would not forsake them, even though some of them criticized him and questioned the authenticity of his ministry.

In all that he suffered, Paul was determined to be what he was supposed to be in the eyes of God. He never stopped being honest with people. He confronted their sin (even if it caused them sorrow), and he never turned away from his God-given responsibility to them. Paul held his ground and never gave up. Whatever it took, Paul did it, but always within the confines of the biblical truth he believed and lived.

Strong words from the prophet Amos epitomize where we are as a nation today.

> "Behold, the days are coming," says the Lord God,
> "That I will send a famine on the land,
> Not a famine of bread,
> Nor a thirst for water,
> But of hearing the words of the Lord.
> They shall wander from sea to sea,
> And from north to east;
> They shall run to and fro, seeking the word of the Lord,
> But shall not find it.
> In that day the fair virgins
> And strong young men
> Shall faint from thirst" (Amos 8:11-13).

We all need to determine if we are floating with the currents of our culture or swimming upstream against them. Any dead fish can float with the current, but it takes a *live one* to swim upstream!

We often try too hard to figure things out for ourselves, and in the process complicate our lives to the point where we can't distinguish truth from error. We become so busy trying to transform our lives and the lives of others that we neglect the simple act of laying our lives bare before the Lord, asking Him to have His way. In this self-improvement culture that looks to yoga, counseling, and amateur psychology for help in changing ourselves and diagnosing the problems of others, we tend to forget that way back in Isaiah our Lord Jesus Christ was called "Wonderful, Counselor, Mighty God, Everlasting Father, Prince of Peace" (9:6b). Job writes, "With Him are wisdom and strength, He has counsel and understanding" (12:13). In the Psalms it is written, "I will instruct you and teach you in the way you should go; I will guide you with My eye" (32:8).

Surprisingly, the New Testament has nothing to say about counsel and counselors, with the exception of the counsel of God, or of people taking counsel against someone, as in the crucifixion story. We have "the mind of Christ" since Jesus ascended into heaven and sent us the comforter, His Holy Spirit. We neglect the wealth of the wisdom of God at our peril when we neglect to hear and obey His Word and His voice. What results is a poverty of choice.

This is not to say that we don't benefit from the godly input of others. If a dozen people are telling you the same thing, then you'd better listen. If it's a "rogue voice", pray about it and follow God, not man. The Bible is about relationships from start to finish, and He has set up a divine plan for our protection and growth. It is God Himself who teaches us and heals us through His Spirit, and He often chooses to use people to do that. There is no place in the Word of God that better explains this than Ephesians 4:11-16.

> And He Himself gave some to be apostles, some prophets, some evangelists, and some pastors and teachers, for the *equipping of the saints* for the work of ministry, for the edifying of the body of Christ, *till we all come to the unity of the faith and of the knowledge of the Son of God, to a perfect man, to the measure of the stature of the fullness of Christ; that we should no longer be children*, tossed to and fro and carried about with every wind of doctrine, by the trickery of men, in the cunning craftiness of deceitful plotting, but, *speaking the truth in love, may grow up in all things into Him who is the head – Christ –* from whom the whole body, joined and knit together by what every joint supplies, according to the effective working by every part does its share, *causes growth of the body for the edifying of itself in love* (emphasis mine).

There is only One whom we need to please at all times—our Lord Jesus Christ. He alone is full of grace and truth, but we should strive to achieve balance as well. I know that I am often more full of truth than grace, and I continually pray that God will "grow me" in grace. However, I never want to sacrifice truth *for* grace. Even though Paul was considered unnecessarily harsh at times, he wasn't swayed or influenced by the opinions of others. When it comes to difficult circumstances in our lives, may we follow Paul's example no matter what the personal cost. May we live what we believe and grow in grace.

There is nothing in the word of God that indicates we have to go through all of our trials publicly. If someone is pressuring us with anything that God is not, we should continue to pray and move on to reach out to those to whom God is leading us to minister. "We ought to obey God rather than men" (Acts 5:29b).

David writes in the Psalms, "Lord, all my desire is before You; And my sighing is not hidden from You" (38:9). Our deepest passions and desires are no secret to God, even when they remain a secret to us. He is far more aware of them than we are. When Jesus said, "If anyone is thirsty, let him come to me and drink" (John 7:37), He knew the people He spoke to were all thirsty, but He knew they weren't aware of their thirst.

During those three difficult years after I began to pray for passion in my life, I suffered an excruciating kidney-stone attack. I knew what it was when it hit, because I'd had one about twenty years earlier. After an extremely painful ordeal in the hospital, where the stone was pulverized by ultrasonic lithotripsy, my doctor advised me to drink a lot of water. I've never liked to drink water unless I feel *really* thirsty. The doctor tried to convince me that, whether I felt thirsty or not, I had to drink, drink, drink.

"Am I supposed to carry a water bottle around with me all the time?" I asked.

The doctor peered at me over the top of his glasses. "Only if you drink from it," he said. "Otherwise, it's useless!"

How many of us are like this in our spiritual lives? We need the Living Water desperately, but unless we experience a crisis, we don't "drink" from Him. We carry our Bibles around, but how often do we absorb it so we courageously apply Bible truth? We have the God of the Universe accessible to us twenty-four hours a day, but how often do we draw from *His* power? How often do we spend time with Him just deepening and developing our love relationship?

Jesus kept the solution extremely simple. All He said was, "If anyone thirsts, let him *come to Me* and drink" (John 7:37, emphasis mine). In the very next two verses He says, "He who believes in Me, as the Scripture has said, out from his heart will flow rivers of living water. But this He spoke concerning the Spirit, whom those believing in Him would receive" (7:38-39b), referring to the Holy Spirit who was soon to come. We waste a great deal of time trying to satisfy our unmet longings and desires. But without Jesus, there is no lasting solution. When we *come* to Jesus with those longings, we show that we trust Him and are becoming women after His heart. This is *faith.*

We are told in Hebrews 11:1, "Now faith is the substance of things hoped for, the evidence of things not seen." Both the Old and New Testaments remind us that the just shall live by faith (Romans 1:17b, Habakkuk 2:4b).

As the children of Israel wandered around in the desert for forty years, there were times when they were parched with thirst and there was no water in sight. At one of these times God told Moses, "Gather the people together, and I will give them water" (Numbers 21:16). Did dark clouds gather? Did water fall from the sky? No. Did Moses hit a rock to release a miraculous stream of water? Not this time. The people gathered in circles on the sand and *by faith* used their rods and sticks to dig a hole in the hot sand. As they did this they sang, "Spring up, O well! All of you sing to it —" (21:17), and with that, gurgling water rose from the underground stream to fill the well, and it flowed along the arid ground!

It sounds crazy, doesn't it? But what a beautiful picture of what God wants us to do with the barren and thirsty places in our lives. Our praises will open fountains in the desert as we come to Him with believing, expectant hearts. There is nothing that pleases God more than a heart of praise, and nothing that displeases Him more than grumbling, bitterness and an unforgiving spirit. Are you thanking Him for His countless blessings in your life and recognizing that He allows all trials, struggles, and tests for a purpose? Are you expecting a positive outcome *before* you praise Him? Again, this is *faith.*

The Scriptures have a lot to say about God's desire for us to be passionate for Him. Not cold, not lukewarm, but *hot.* When we lose sight of the truth that only Jesus can meet the deepest longings of our hearts, we move from true Christianity into legalism and religiosity. We were created for love and for relationships. As we look through God's Word, we see that the entire story of man, from Genesis to Revelation, is a journey of relationships and families. God longs for us to give our hearts to Him, to "fall in love" with Him, because He loves us. A woman after God's heart is a woman with a passion, a longing for God. The example used throughout the Bible is an excited bride and bridegroom waiting for their wedding day. There has never been a romance novel written that can compare with the love story of all love stories born in the heart of God. The more honest and obedient we are with Him, the more God fills those empty places in our lives and we find the passionate love our hearts thirst for.

Even though we live in a culture that continually tells us to bite our lip and smile when the pain gets unbearable, it's okay to hurt. We often medicate our pain through busyness, jobs, shopping, sleeping, eating, television and computers, education, hobbies, sports and recreation, reading, medication, addictive substances, or whatever brings us momentary happiness. Instead of patiently trusting God as we pray and wait on His timing, we become angry and bitter. Simply put, we do an expert job of making ourselves, and others, miserable.

First, we must realize that perfect happiness is impossible in this life. We are not dealing with perfect people, perfect relationships, or a perfect world. There isn't one of us who hasn't felt disappointed in every close relationship we have ever had, and there is a hollow vacuum within us the size of the Grand Canyon that can only be filled satisfactorily by one thing: the God who created us. He speaks tenderly to that empty part of us, even while we scramble to fill it with everything but Him.

All of us have passions, even though we tend to shy away from using such a strong word to describe them. Some of our longings and desires are acceptable, and some aren't. Beginning with Eve in the book of Genesis, we see person after person running amok by following the lies of the world, the flesh or the devil. They all thought they were missing something. That hasn't changed between then and now. God seems to delight in having us postpone complete satisfaction till heaven, which involves seemingly endless waiting, and we don't like to wait.

As I struggled with regaining the passion that was missing in my life, I discovered God's secret for being victorious in times of waiting. I found that waiting is God's forge for purifying us so that His image can be seen in us. "For you have need of endurance, so that after you have done the will of God, you may receive the promise" (Hebrews 10:36). Instead of letting Him accomplish His perfect work in us on His timetable, we usually decide to take matters into our own hands. When we're disappointed and feel let down, it's easy to become bitter and angry, but "stuffing it" only makes us depressed ... or worse. Depression is often simply the difference between expectation and reality.

When I feel weak, disappointed, or depressed, it is invariably because I have lost my joy. There is a wonderful verse in Nehemiah that says, "Do not sorrow, for *the joy of the Lord is your strength*" (8:10b, emphasis mine). Happiness is dependent on circumstances; joy is not. True joy is found only in the Lord.

Trusting Him in faith is the bottom line. If He truly fails to come through for me, then I am a goner and have no hope whatsoever. This is the recognition that leads to change. It is the lesson God spoke to my heart when I cried out to Him for passion in my life, and it is simple enough for a child to understand. Hear His words and obey. The rest is His responsibility. Our fear of change needs to be less than our fear of a mediocre, lukewarm, second-rate life for God. Once we realize that, we will begin to grow and move toward maturity in our walk with God.

Points to Ponder and Pray

Do you miss passion in your life? Are there any dry, parched places in your life that desperately need the water of life? Have you determined that you are ready to come to Jesus with your longings, disappointments, and pain? Then stop right here for a few moments simply to tell God exactly what is on your heart.

Tabernacle Truth

In 1996 I was asked by my church to lead an in-depth Bible study on the Tabernacle using *A Woman's Heart: God's Dwelling Place* (Beth Moore, Nashville, TN: LifeWay Press). During that study, God showed me that the messages He had given me for my Passionate Hearts conferences fit perfectly into this visual of the Tabernacle, which He had prepared thousands of years ago. The Tabernacle provides a clear picture of how we can make our way into the Holy of Holies and intimacy with God!

There are about fifty chapters in the Bible that refer to the Old Testament Tabernacle, which seems to indicate how important God thought it was. It was the very first place in history that God chose to inhabit and live among His people. It was located in what is now northwest Saudi Arabia, on Jebel El Lawz, the highest peak in a mountain range. God's people arrived at Mount Sinai after they crossed the Red Sea, which is today called the Gulf of Aqaba and separates the Sinai Peninsula (Egypt) and Saudi Arabia, a distance of about eight miles across. (Amazing video segments of this and other exciting discoveries in the Middle East can be viewed in the "Presentation of Discoveries" video and/or booklet. See the appendix for information.)

The Tabernacle was a two-part tent with an outer courtyard area surrounded by a fence. (Diagrams of the structure and its furnishings are included in the appendix.) This physical structure was an Old Testament example of a New Testament truth. Every single part of the Tabernacle was a symbol of the coming Messiah, our Lord Jesus Christ. (For a deeper understanding of the Tabernacle, read Exodus in the Old Testament and Hebrews in the New Testament.)

Each of the three areas of the Tabernacle—the Outer Court, the Holy Place (or sanctuary), and the Holy of Holies— is symbolic of the steps necessary to establish an intimate relationship with God. There is only *one way* to intimacy with God, and there are no shortcuts.

There were many times throughout the history of Israel, as portrayed in the first five books of the Bible, where the people trembled with fear and withdrew. Even so, God did not desert them. He gave them the Law, the commandments, directions for building an altar, and the pattern for worship in the wilderness Tabernacle. When they left Mount Sinai carrying the Ark Of The Covenant, they knew beyond the shadow of a doubt that God was among them. Are we any different? Certainly not. All who respond to the call from Sinai, who come to the mountain in faithful obedience, will leave with the blessed assurance that God is with them.

We can meet God on the mountain only because Jesus has perfectly fulfilled the requirements of the Law. As Christians we don't have to make a pilgrimage to the geographical location of Sinai (even though you can have that amazing experience anytime by video), but we have a meeting with Him in our heart. As we encounter the presence of Almighty God, every fiber of our being will come under his probing gaze. Jehovah God wants to open our lives and fill us with His very own life, but He leaves that decision up to us. Never will He force His presence, His love, or His power on us. The choice is up to us. Will we allow our selfish human nature to drive us in fear from the Lord or will we submit to Him? God *will* work miraculously. *All He requires is trust and obedience.* As the old saying goes, "Trust and obey or you'll rust and decay."

I will attempt to walk you through my journey into intimacy with God in this book, beginning at the gate and ending in the Holy of Holies. As we go, you can pinpoint where you are in your own personal journey. This book is not written chronologically, but rather draws on relevant experiences pulled out of over half a century of my life.

God said He would commune with His people in the Holy of Holies, that last and deepest part of the Tabernacle. Will you join me on this journey?

Chapter 1

The Gate is Wide Enough for You

Was I born with a silver spoon in my mouth? No. But then, a stainless steel spoon is nothing to complain about. I am incredibly blessed to have come into a home with both a mother *and* a father who loved me. However, my twenty-one-month-old brother, Gary, wasn't so sure. The day I arrived home from the hospital he admonished my parents to "take her back!" (I don't think he changed his mind until we were in high school and he began to date my friends.)

When I was eighteen months old, Gary and I welcomed our new baby brother, Tommy, into our little family. This new arrival turned out to be one of my best friends as we grew up. We even attended Arizona State University together for a couple of years.

I was almost eight and finishing up the second grade before Robin, brother number three, arrived on the scene. At that age I thought it only fair that my parents provide me with a sister who would help even out the odds at home. But the minute I saw his angelic little face, my disappointment evaporated. From that day forward I was delighted to be his second mother.

Nine months before I was born, I began attending church on a weekly basis. If regular church attendance was the requirement to enter heaven, I had nothing to worry about. When I was a month old, I was dutifully taken to the church to be baptized before God and many witnesses. If baptism proved to be the requirement to enter heaven, I had that base covered as well.

What about the Ten Commandments, God's "Top Ten List"? Well, I wasn't too bad. In my opinion, I had a solid 51 percent nailed at least. If good works were the requirement to enter heaven, I had no serious concerns there either.

My parents met each other at a church college in Minnesota. They, as well as their parents and their parents' parents, had all grown up in church. If God had grandchildren, I was well on my way.

By the time I was eight years old, I figured I had my ticket to heaven already punched. But then one night, I woke up with a terrifying nightmare about falling into a bottomless black pit. Somehow I knew it represented an eternity without hope. Hearing my screams, my mother came into my bedroom to comfort me, but to no avail.

It continually amazes me that God, in His mercy, heard the cry of a little girl's heart on that night, as He still does today. Whether I am eight, eighteen, or eighty, I am "God's little girl." The following summer, on my ninth birthday, I heard the Good News of Jesus Christ for the first time during a Vacation Bible School across town from my own church. There I learned that God's requirement and promise for eternal life. The Gospel of John states it clearly in chapter three, in one of the best-known passages of the Bible:

> That whoever believes in Him should not perish but have eternal life. For God so loved the world that he gave His only begotten Son, that whoever believes in Him should not perish but have everlasting life. For God did not send His Son into the world to condemn the world, but that the world through Him might be saved. He who believes in Him is not condemned; but he who does not believe is condemned already, because he has not believed in the name of the only begotten Son of God (John 3:15-18).

On June 11, 1956, I learned that Jesus Christ had been crucified on a Roman cross to pay the penalty for my sins. I received that payment personally by repenting of my sin and inviting Him to be my personal Lord and Savior. I was "reborn" that day. I celebrate my physical birthday and my spiritual birthday on the same day. From that day to this, I have been certain of forgiveness and eternal life with Him in heaven. I have never doubted my eternal destination because I settled with God at the "altar of sacrifice" and determined that I would accept His perfect sacrifice for my sins. My only other option was to spend eternity apart from Him because of my inability to save myself.

Tabernacle Truth

You may be hanging around outside the gate of the Tabernacle, not sure how to enter in. This is where I spent the first nine years of my life. Our symbolic journey through the Tabernacle begins by entering at the gate.

The actual Tabernacle gate was a fenced-in area facing east. It was 150 feet long, 75 feet wide, and $7^{1/2}$ feet high. White linen hung all along the fence, except on the gate, which had 30 feet of blue-and-scarlet linen. (Please refer to the appendix for diagrams.)

As I said, every part of the Tabernacle is an Old Testament picture or symbol of a New Testament truth. The gate is no exception.

In John 10:9a Jesus said, "I am the door. If anyone enters by Me, he will be saved." In chapters 9-10 of John, Jesus makes it clear that He alone is the door.

Remember the story of Noah? When destruction was coming to the earth, Noah brought his family and the pairs of living creatures safely on board the ark. Then God closed the door. Jesus is our ark of safety, our gate into the holy Tabernacle.

Have you entered in at the narrow gate? "Enter by the narrow gate; for wide is the gate and broad is the way that leads to destruction, and there are many who go in by it. Because narrow is the gate and difficult is the way which leads to life, and there are few who find it" (Matthew 7:13). But no matter how narrow the door, it's wide enough for you. Just as with the father of the prodigal son in Luke 15, when Jesus sees you coming He will run to meet you with arms outstretched in love.

This may be your last opportunity to settle the question of where you will spend eternity. There are only two options. Will you accept the perfect sacrifice of Jesus' death on the cross for your sins or will you try to pay for your sins yourself? The Bible makes it clear that the latter requires an eternity of separation from God. While I am not trying to exercise scare tactics, I am sounding the clarion call of warning, just as Jesus did.

When Jesus was on earth, He talked more about hell than He did about heaven. "And as it is appointed for men to die once, but after this the judgment, so Christ was offered once to bear the sins of many. To those who eagerly wait for Him He will appear a second time, apart from sin, for salvation" (Hebrews 9:27-28).

Some people think they are right with God, but they are seriously mistaken. "Not everyone who says to Me, 'Lord, Lord,' shall enter the kingdom of heaven … And then I will declare to them, 'I never knew you; depart from Me, you who practice lawlessness!'" (Matthew 7:21a, 23). We must all go to the root of our sin problem, both the sin nature we have had since birth and the daily sins we practice by choice. Once the struggle over who you are in relation to a holy God is settled, the struggle ceases and life begins.

If you haven't come to the point of knowing Jesus Christ personally, you haven't been born again spiritually. All you have to do is turn to Him right now and ask. He is not as concerned with your words as He is with the attitude of your heart. You can pray a prayer similar to this one:

> Lord Jesus, I want to know You personally. Thank You for dying on the cross for my sins. I open the door of my life and receive You as my Savior and Lord. Thank You for forgiving all my sins—no matter how horrible they have been—and for giving me the free gift of eternal life. Please take control of my life and make me the kind of person You want me to be.

Once we come to know Christ personally, Jesus reminds us in John 13:8b, "If I do not wash you, you have no part with Me."

It is impossible to have intimacy with God if there is sin in our lives that we aren't willing to part with, whether it is an attitude, action, or habit. God promises us in 1 John 1:9 that "If we confess our sins, He is faithful and just to forgive us our sins and to cleanse us from all unrighteousness." There is absolutely nothing that He will not forgive.

As we lay the sin down, God will multiply blessings in our lives. God gives an amazing promise in Isaiah 61:7.

"Instead of your shame you shall have double honor,
And instead of confusion they shall rejoice in their portion.
Therefore in their land they shall possess double;
Everlasting joy shall be theirs."

Brokenness breaks the curse of barrenness in our lives. As we take this step we see the power and life of the crucified, risen Lord Jesus begin to flow through us. Not only does our intimate relationship with Him begin, but only then can He use us to reach out to others who desperately need Him.

Many people don't want to be transformed; they want to be translated. Who knows what we give up in order to compromise? We must take a stand. We've got to have a revival of morality. It requires change. Satan is the god of this world system, and it's truly amazing to watch the worldly games that people play to get things. God is looking for people to promote, to lift up.

Forgiveness requires repentance. Not jailhouse repentance – "I'm sorry I got caught" – but rather "I want to do whatever it takes to never do it again". Don't try to run away from God, because He will just send someone else to try to get our attention. Let's not be hypocrites. Let's *do* what we *believe* and be uncompromisingly righteous. Nobody wants to be around a "yo-yo" Christian who is up and down all the time. Let's care more about later on than right now. God will change us if we cooperate with Him.

Let's not run in the flesh, but walk in the Spirit. We can't change ourselves, but we *can* change. The words of God are spirit and life. We must depend on Him to change us. We need to get over being independent. We should act desperate before we get desperate. Remember that we are "pruned" if we do and "pruned" if we don't! "Every branch in Me that does not bear fruit He takes away; and every branch that bears fruit He prunes, that it may bear more fruit" (John 15:2).

If God blessed His children in disobedience, they would never be provoked to get out of it. If we stay full of hope, Satan cannot stop us. Hope is a positive expectancy of good things happening in our future, whereas disobedience is the cause of a miserable life. Never forget that there is no pit so deep that God is not deeper still.

There is no place for repeat or defeat in God's program. Free choice is what makes us all created equal. Let's not live in the past. We need to move on and stop feeling sorry for ourselves and being "pity-full." No one comes to our pity parties except us, anyway. We need to get over it and stop complaining. As we begin to look at someone else's sores, we'll forget about our own. We must leave our concerns with God because change is only possible through the power of His Holy Spirit anyway. Anyone who consistently makes right choices will be blessed. We *can* reverse the curse.

"If anyone desires to come after Me, let him deny himself, and take up his cross, and follow Me. For whoever desires to save his life will lose it, but whoever loses his life for My sake will find it. For what profit is it to a man if he gains the whole world, and loses his own soul? Or what will a man give in exchange for his soul? For the Son of Man will come in the glory of His Father with His angels, and then He will reward each according to his works" (Matthew 16:24-27).

Jesus didn't come to give us a comfortable life; He came to give us an abundant life. Remember that God called Shadrach, Meshach, and Abed Nego *into* the fiery furnace, He called Daniel *into* the lion's den, He called Jonah *into* the great fish, and He called Joseph *into* the pit and the prison. We will have trials whether we choose to go with God or not. We live in a fallen and sinful world. The good news is that with God there is purpose in every trial that He allows to come into our lives.

"Therefore humble yourselves under the mighty hand of God, that He may exalt you in due time, casting all your care upon Him, for He cares for you. Be sober, be vigilant; because your adversary the devil walks about like a roaring lion, seeking whom he may devour. Resist him, steadfast in the faith, knowing that the same sufferings are experienced by your brotherhood in the world. But may the God of all grace, who called us to His eternal glory by Christ Jesus, after you have suffered a while, perfect, establish, strengthen, and settle you" (First Peter 5:10).

We're not called to be achievers; we're called to be believers. "Did you receive the Spirit by the works of the law, or by the hearing of faith? Are you so foolish? Having begun in the Spirit, are you now being made perfect by the flesh? … just as Abraham 'believed God, and it was accounted to him for righteousness'" (Galatians 3:2b-3, 6).

Whether we have been born with the proverbial silver spoon, a stainless steel spoon, a plastic spoon, or no spoon in our mouth, makes no eternal difference. What matters is that we understand how to tap into all the riches available to us by our Father, our Abba (Daddy), as we become part of His family. "But as many as received Him, to them He gave the right to become children of God, to those who believe in His name; who were born ... of God" (John 1:12, 13b).

Points to Ponder and Pray

Be cautious about getting overly excited when someone tells you that they are a "born again Christian". These people are defined in surveys as people who say they have made a personal commitment to Jesus Christ and that He is still important in their life today. They also say that they know they will go to heaven after they die because they have confessed their sins and accepted Jesus Christ as their Savior.

A recent study from the Barna Research Group on "The State of the Church in the U.S." shows some chilling results of what those surveyed actually believe and practice.

1) 47% believe that Satan is just a symbol of evil rather than a living being
2) 31% believe that if a person is good enough they can earn a place in heaven
3) 26% believe that it doesn't matter what faith you follow because they all teach the same lessons
4) 24% believe that Jesus committed sins just like other people
5) 15% believe that Jesus did not return to life physically after He was crucified and died
6) 95% have never led one person to Christ
7) 34% gave any time and/or money to serve the poor in the last year
8) 27% have experienced divorce (compared to 24% of non born again people)
9) 16% gave no money to his/her church in the last year and only 8% tithed to their church
10) 7 times more time spent on entertainment than on spiritual activities

11) 30% watched an "R" rated movie in the last week (compared to 40% of non born again people)
12) None said the single most important goal in their life was to be a committed follower of Jesus Christ

Had there been any other way for you to get to heaven, Jesus would not have had to die for your sins. It is made clear throughout the Bible that there is only one way to God, and that is through the sacrificial death of Jesus Christ. He was the perfect Lamb of God who was given by God to take away the sin of the world. (The gospel of John is an excellent place to read if you would like to get a better understanding of this truth.) The following questions are the most important ones you will ever have to answer.

First, if you were to die tonight, do you have assurance that Jesus Christ has paid the penalty for your sins, that you have received His gift of salvation by faith, and that you would spend eternity with God? Remember, no matter how narrow the door may be it is wide enough for you.

Second, if you came to the Lord, but are not living in obedience and purity as His bride, do you now desire to come back to your "first love"? He already knows your heart, and is "bending down His ear to hear you" right now. You'll know if He has received You because His Spirit will put a hunger for God's Word into your life. Unless you have this hunger for the Bible, you might be trying to spruce up the same old flesh life that will never please God. "Weekend at Bernie's" is a film about two young men who were invited to a weekend in a fabulous beach home owned by Bernie, a new friend of theirs. Unfortunately, just before they arrived, Bernie had been "done in" by a hit man. As they realized that their host was dead, and realizing that they were the prime suspects in his murder, they figured that all they could do was to assure everyone that Bernie was still alive until they could get away. The two guys made strenuous and hilarious efforts to show onlookers that Bernie was still alive. They put sunglasses and a hat on his corpse. They sat him out by the pool. They ferried him around in his motorboat and even took him water skiing to make him look full of life, but it was all a sham. Bernie had no life. All he had was the appearance of life. Sadly, many who call themselves Christians, show as much spiritual life as Bernie, but would rather not deal with their lack of interest in the things of God so they try to "look" at a distance, like a committed follower of Jesus even though there's no clear evidence of spiritual life and vitality.

What is the character of the new person in Christ? Love people as Jesus loved them. Any time the word of God tells you to do something, you have the power to do it.

> "Therefore, as the elect of God, holy and beloved, put on tender mercies, kindness, humility, meekness, longsuffering; bearing with one another, and forgiving one another, if anyone has a complaint against another; even as Christ forgave you, so you also must do. But above all these things put on love, which is the bond of perfection. And let the peace of God rule in your hearts, to which also you were called in one body; and be thankful. Let the word of Christ dwell in you richly in all wisdom, teaching and admonishing one another in psalms and hymns and spiritual songs, singing with grace in your hearts to the Lord. And whatever you do in word or deed, do all in the name of the Lord Jesus, giving thanks to God the Father through Him" (Colossians 3:12-17).

"Lord, help me to live what I preach. Don't let me be deceived. The world is getting so confusing, so please help me to keep my nose in the Book. Fill me with your gifts. Please show up and have Your way in my life."

If you feel God calling you to a new life of obedience and you don't really know where to start, I encourage you to pray the prayers of the New Testament, inserting your own name into them. From there extend those prayers to those around you. God *will* answer and begin to open the windows of heaven for you.

Please make sure you have settled your eternal destiny with God before turning the page.

Chapter 2

Daughter of the King

As I stood there on the stage at the Mountain Shadows Resort and Country Club in Scottsdale, Arizona anxiously awaiting the judges' decision, my body ran a triathlon of sorts – head swimming, heart racing, body sweating. The winner's name sounded oddly like my own. Wait, they *were* calling my name! "And now, Miss Wool of Arizona 1969 — Laurie Steen!" As I walked across that stage toward the lovely young woman who had won the crown the previous year, I couldn't believe she was extending it to me. I would wear that crown for a year, with all the privileges and responsibilities that came with the title.

I'm sure there are very few little girls who don't, at one time or another, dream of being a princess. Even though I was a confirmed tomboy growing up with three brothers and no sisters, I secretly clung to my romantic notions of one day being part of a Cinderella-like fairy tale. Aside from high school crowns of cardboard, spray paint, and glitter, this was the closest I had ever come to looking and feeling like true royalty.

I was a twenty-one-year old coed at Arizona State University at the time. It had been twelve years since I was born into God's family, and I had been walking closely with Jesus Christ for over three years, but I grasped very little of the truth that I was actually a daughter of the King of Kings, a *true* princess.

The Bible has a lot to say about becoming a child of God. One of the first verses I ever memorized is John 1:12: "But as many as received Him, to them He gave the right to become children of God, to those who believe in His name." Even now, after being in His family for over forty years, I still have a hard time wrapping my mind around the fact that God is my Father and I am His little girl.

How is it possible that I could be a real princess, the daughter of the King of Kings? It is not in my feeble prayer asking Him to be my Father, but in simply receiving His Son, who died for me.

Tabernacle Truth

After we enter the Tabernacle through the gate, we come into the Outer Court. There, near the entrance, stands the Brazen Altar—the great altar for the sacrifice of animals, standing $7^{1/2}$ feet square and $4^{1/2}$ feet high, built of acacia wood and covered with brass. The altar itself is hollow but filled in with earth. God miraculously kindled the fire on it and it was never to burn out. God alone is responsible for lighting the fire by His divine hand. Only fire originating from Him can truly purify or approve an offering. God lights the fire, while His people are responsible for keeping it fueled.

During that period of history, the altar was where the sacrifice was slain. It pictures for us the reality that we have no way to God except by the blood of His sacrificial Lamb, our Lord Jesus Christ. Forgiveness is God's part in the exchange, but participation is up to us.

If we could get to God any other way than through the cross of Jesus Christ, then His death was unnecessary. The priest had to take the blood from the altar into the Holy of Holies once a year to pay the penalty for the sins of the Israelites. Justification and forgiveness remain supernatural miracles of God's grace and work rather than us being sorry for our sins or even repenting, but because of what our Lord and Savior Jesus Christ has done for us. When we approach the altar believing that Christ died for us, instantly His death places us in right relationship with God, and every sin is forgiven.

The single most important decision I can make in my lifetime is whether I choose to accept the perfect sacrifice of Jesus' death on the cross for my sins, or try to pay for them myself. The Scriptures make it clear that the latter choice requires an eternity of suffering and separation from God in hell. This is an impossible undertaking because we can never make perfect what is already imperfect. Just as it only takes one drop of contaminated water to pollute a beaker full of pure water, if we have only sinned once in our lives, we are guilty. The book of Romans makes clear that "all have sinned and fall short of the glory of God" (3:23), and the book of James points out, "For whoever shall keep the whole law, and yet stumble in one point, he is guilty of all" (2:10).

Our daughter Trinity, as a young teenager, wrote a letter to her Hollywood "heart throb" at the time, Leonardo DiCaprio, which explains my point more clearly than anything else I know. With her permission, I offer it to you in part:

> ***Dear Leonardo,***
> ***I don't think you will be the one reading this because since you get so much mail, other people probably help read it. I just wanted to tell you about something that changed my life. You seem to have it all: good career, great family (I don't know them, but you seem to like them), millions of girls dying to meet or even go out with you (including me), money $$$$, etc., but there is something missing. It's a relationship with the One who made you and loves you more than anyone on this earth, no matter what you've done. He got nails driven through His hands and feet, spit on, mocked and beaten so badly you couldn't even have recognized Him, all because He didn't want to spend eternity without you. He died for everyone, but if you were the only person on this earth, He still would have done it.***
> ***I have enclosed a booklet that explains this. Please read it! I'll tell you what happened with me now. I seemed to have everything too: good looks, good grades, great family, lots of friends and hopefully a modeling career in the future, but I still didn't feel complete. Jesus was what I was missing. When I asked Him to come into my life, I felt complete and full of a joy that I can't describe. I don't know you personally, but you seem like a great guy; loyal, a sense of humor, and an awesome actor. I took the time to write this letter because I don't want you to go to hell when you die. God wants you to live with Him in heaven for eternity. If you have any questions, just write me. I wouldn't mind!***
> ***I'll be praying 4 U,***
> ***Trinity***

My earthly reign as a "princess" lasted for only one year, but my eternal reign as the daughter of the King will continue for eternity. The only kingdom that will prevail in this world is the kingdom that is not of this world. In this transient world of the temporary, what amazing security comes with the permanence of God's promises. The entrance fee into the kingdom of God was paid by Jesus' blood. The kingdom of God does not exist because we are His subjects. It exists because the King of Kings reigns. Our part is to enter this kingdom and bring our life under His sovereign will. The powers of the kingdom of God in the age to come are operative even today.

The promises and rewards of being a part of the "royal family" are waiting to be discovered between the covers of our Bibles. Not only did He give us sixty-six books in this "library", but He also gives us the indwelling Holy Spirit Who gives us the power to live and walk in the truths we find there. It is impossible for our earthly children to obey us if they don't know what is expected of them. So it is with our Father. As we obey Him and walk in the power of the His Spirit by faith, He unveils the great adventure for which He created us.

There are stories in the Bible of queens who got it right and those who got it wrong. To see the difference that they made for both good and evil is a real eye-opener. There are about twenty mentioned in the Old Testament and six in the New Testament. The word is given about fifty times in Scripture. Of all of these women, Esther is my favorite. There is an entire book in the Bible named for her and it would be well worth your reading. You will also be learning more about her life as you progress on your personal journey through the Tabernacle.

As I think about ruling and reigning with Christ for all eternity, my mind immediately goes to the "last chapter." If you would like to get a picture of how this real-life fairy tale plays out, go to the last book in your Bible, Revelation, and read chapters 21 and 22. "Surely I am coming quickly. Amen. Even so, come, Lord Jesus!" (22:20)

Points to Ponder and Pray

If you are weary of the impossible task of trying to be good enough to please a holy God, and you are now ready to come into the permanent relationship of becoming His forever child, I encourage you to reread chapters 1 and 2 before continuing. If you would like additional help in understanding God's requirement for salvation, read the Gospel of John in the Bible.

If you would like some help on your journey and know someone who is a growing Christian, would you put this book down long enough to give them a call? I am confident this person would be delighted to hear from you.

If you do not belong to a strong, Bible-teaching church, don't wait to be invited. Look for a solid Bible believing church and begin to attend regularly.

Chapter 3

Hanging Around the Altar

As I dug my knees into the bare back of the hard charging horse beneath my body and clung desperately to the reins, I knew I was in big trouble. What was I thinking? The animal wasn't even fully broken yet, and there I was, a seventeen-year-old novice, out for an afternoon of adventure without so much as a saddle. As Thunder galloped across the meadow at breakneck speed, I noticed a creek looming ahead. On the far side, low-hanging boughs of a large tree covered the path. I had to make a split-second decision. Whatever I did in the next instant could determine whether or not I'd spend the rest of my life in a wheelchair.

As Thunder vaulted the creek, I let go of the reins, thinking the water would afford a soft cushion for my falling body. Little did I know that several large boulders waited for me just beneath the surface. As I hit, excruciating pain shot through my right arm and ribs. The horse, having dispatched his unwelcome rider, came to an abrupt halt on the far side of the creek under the low-hanging boughs. He turned to face me with eyes blazing, the loose hanging reins snapping like a bullwhip as he repeatedly tossed his head, nostrils flaring.

After struggling to get back on my feet, I surveyed the damage to my body. Lacerations covered my right side, but I felt most of the pain on the inside. I had never experienced agony like that in all of my seventeen years.

I waded across the creek and up the opposite bank, where I retrieved the reins and began limping back to the barn. "Why did I take this job in the first place?" I lamented, my ribs throbbing with every jarring step. "What made me think working as a housekeeper and cook for a wealthy elderly couple at their ranch would be fun?" The Smiths hired Daryl, my good friend since second grade, to be the handyman and groundskeeper. It would be our final summer as high school students. I was excited about making $95 a month after three summers of working for my parents for only $30 a month. When I was thirteen, my mom went back to college during the summers to complete her teaching degree and my dad was paid to go to summer school through a National Science Fellowship. I already had a lot of experience with housekeeping, cooking and childcare by the 17th summer of my life, but who knew life on a ranch could be so painful?

When I reached the cabin, I tethered the horse to a fence and dragged myself to my room without taking him back to the pasture. I wanted to take a shower, but felt so faint that I lay down on the cement floor, with no strength to move another inch.

Through the fog of pain in my head, I heard Daryl's frustrated voice shouting at me to put the horse away. I tried calling to him from the shower room floor, but my voice was faint. When he walked in and found me in a pitiful, muddy heap on the floor, he immediately took charge of the situation. He insisted on taking me to the hospital. We were the only ones at "home on the range" that day, so he helped me up and half-dragged me to the big cattle truck, our only means of transportation.

Those were the longest thirty miles I'd ever experienced. Every bump in the road felt like a knife twisting between my ribs.

Daryl finally pulled into the hospital parking lot and I was rushed in for X-rays. Thank the Lord, the doctor reported no broken bones. But I couldn't go back to my job at the ranch right away. I returned home to my family, where I recuperated for a few days before going back to the ranch to finish out my summer.

My wild ride on that horse is an example of my search for satisfaction and excitement as a teenager. All of the exploits from my senior year alone would take up an entire book. This hunger for excitement started when I was a young child, but escalated over the years. During the summer before my final year in high school, I danced around the edge of danger, and then started down a slippery slope that lasted that entire year. I let my standards slip in many areas. I started dating guys much older than I, became an addicted smoker, indulged in alcohol socially, partied and caroused every weekend, and lied to my parents to cover my tracks. During that year, deceit became an art form.

After we come into God's family, our lives change. "If anyone is in Christ, he is a new creation; old things have passed away; behold, all things have become new" (2 Corinthians 5:17). Even though my belief system changed at the age of nine, the way I lived that out in a practical way came much more slowly. I was fully alive, just as a newborn baby is alive, but I wasn't fully grown. Ever since the day I became a part of God's kingdom I have been learning what it means to live in the privilege, and the responsibility, of becoming more like Jesus. Without the power of His Holy Spirit within me, however, that is impossible.

Just as we are born once physically, we are also only born once spiritually. To be honest, there are days when I don't feel like a child of God and days when I don't act like one, either. As I near the end of raising five children to become "legal adults," I admit there are days when I want everyone to know they are my children, and days when I struggle to admit that they belong to me at all. These feelings, however, are irrelevant. They have been my children since birth (one since adoption) and they always will be. As I was growing up, I'm sure there were days when my parents would have gladly traded me in for a "different model," yet I am still their daughter.

At the age of seventeen, I was, metaphorically speaking, running in a very large pasture. It had a fence, but what I really needed was a corral. At that age I had no idea how to move into intimacy with God. I attended church weekly in a place where the Bible was rarely mentioned. It took another year before I understood how to move on to the "Brazen Laver" for cleansing.

I followed my conscience as to what was right or wrong (Romans 2:14-15). I believed I was that person with the "good" and "pure" conscience, who genuinely acted in accord with an inner set of godly standards (2 Corinthians 1:12; 1 Timothy 1:5, 19; 3:9). Conscience, however, can be distorted. This inner set of standards is accurate only if it is based on biblical truth. The conscience will be unreliable if faulty standards assimilated by the world around us are consistently accepted as truth. The old saying, "Let your conscience be your guide," only holds true if a person's conscience has been filled with godly principles. This is why Christian parents have the important responsibility of communicating godly standards of right and wrong to their children.

But even a conscience that has been properly nurtured can be disabled. It can become insensitive and calloused if those godly standards change due to peer influence or if a person consistently acts contrary to what he knows is right. I was a babe in Christ, and had no idea how to handle the temptations that came my way. "For everyone who partakes only of milk is unskilled in the word of righteousness, for he is a babe. But solid food belongs to those who are of full age, that is, those who by reason of use have their senses exercised to discern both good and evil" (Hebrews 5:13-14).

Even more serious, the conscience can become "seared" through deliberately choosing to believe the lies of the world, the flesh, or deceiving spirits rather than God's truth. The first chapter of Romans clearly shows the downward spiral that results when we habitually choose to sin. It's not a pretty picture.

Paul also warns us about our walk as believers through the fourth chapter of his letter to the Ephesians. "...that you put off, concerning your former conduct, the old man which grows corrupt according to the deceitful lusts, and be renewed in the spirit of your mind, and that you put on the new man which was created according to God, in true righteousness and holiness" (4:22-24).

In recent years I have begun to understand addictive behavior. As I followed the "pleasure road" that summer before my senior year, I had no idea how quickly those behaviors could become addictive and cause struggles throughout life. The more I repeated a behavior, the more it moved from being a simple pleasure or comfort to an addiction. It is common knowledge that the stages of repeated behaviors develop from habits, to compulsions, to addictions. Apart from God's power and protection, you will find yourself hopelessly entangled in wrong behavior choices.

The sin problem looms much larger than just our actions, since actions spring from within our hearts. This is why the Bible admonishes us to "present your bodies a living sacrifice, holy, acceptable to God, which is your reasonable service. And do not be conformed to this world, but *be transformed by the renewing of your mind*, that you may prove what is that good and acceptable and perfect will of God" (Romans 12:1-2, emphasis mine).

Unconfessed sin in our lives spreads like cancer in the body. It silently and secretly does its deadly work in our lives, until we are virtually useless for the Kingdom of God. Our once white-hot passion for the Lord seems to disappear like the morning fog. No amount of church attendance, Bible reading, counseling, or hanging out with the right people is going to cover sin. Sin must be confessed continually.

Soon after getting involved with Campus Crusade for Christ at Arizona State University as a twenty year old, I learned that I could keep short accounts with God by "spiritual breathing." This process involves exhaling the impure (confession) and inhaling the pure (reappropriating the fullness of the Holy Spirit), that may be done the instant you realize that you have sinned against God in either thought, word, or deed. You may not "feel like it," but feeling forgiven usually follows this act of obedience.

It is incredibly important that we walk in purity and holiness with our God. Though recent presidential campaigns have argued otherwise, character *is* a key issue. Only when we obey Him can we serve as models to our spouses, children, and others. It is imperative that we carefully parent the children God has placed within our homes. (Take a couple of minutes to read Psalm 127 and 128 for a precious picture of how God views children.)

Tabernacle Truth

Once we pass the Altar of Sacrifice, which is the first stop after entering into the Outer Court of the Tabernacle and the symbolic picture of our salvation through Jesus Christ, we come to the Brazen Laver of Cleansing. This, too, was located in the outer courtyard of the Tabernacle just in front of the only entrance into the sanctuary, or Holy Place. The Brazen Laver was a large brass bowl designed to hold water for the priests to wash their hands and feet before they went into the place of service and fellowship.

The Laver is for believers who have dealt with their eternal destiny at the Altar of Sacrifice (the Cross of Christ), yet need to be cleansed daily of their sin. Every sin we commit has been forgiven at the cross of Jesus Christ, but we will not experience fellowship and intimacy with Him unless we are continually walking in purity and obedience with Him.

The inside of the Laver was lined with the mirrors the Israelite women were given as they left Egypt. As the priest approached the Laver each day to wash his hands and feet, he saw his own reflection looking back at him.

What is our mirror? "Therefore lay aside all filthiness and overflow of wickedness, and receive with meekness the implanted word, which is able to save your souls. But be doers of the word, and not hearers only, deceiving yourselves. For if anyone is a hearer of the word and not a doer, he is like a man observing his natural face in a mirror; for he observes himself, goes away, and immediately forgets what kind of man he was. But he who looks into the perfect law of liberty and continues in it, and is not a forgetful hearer but a doer of the work, this one will be blessed in what he does" (James 1:22-25). We are to look intently into the Word of God and abide by what it says. We must examine and cleanse ourselves of whatever sin is hindering us from entering the Holy Place. Jesus said, "If I do not wash you, you have no part with Me" (John 13:8b).

Points to Ponder and Pray

Take some time right now for a "spiritual bath" before you move on to the next chapter. We cannot enter the Holy Place to fellowship or serve without it. "If we confess our sins, He is faithful and just to forgive us our sins and to cleanse us from all unrighteousness" (1 John 1:9). If it helps to have a visible reminder of God's grace, take a sheet of paper and list every sin in your life that He brings to your mind. Once you have asked forgiveness for the sins you have listed and determined to turn from them (repentance), write First John 1:9 across your list and then destroy it. God has forgiven you!

Chapter 4

So What Should I Do?

Every summer since 1991, our family has spent a week or two with our dear friends, the Yelvertons, in South Carolina on the May River near Hilton Head. We put on a Backyard Bible Club, and our children participated as clubbers before the age of twelve and as helpers thereafter. Afternoons were spent swimming, boating, skiing, and diving off the dock.

Time after time I tried to tell the kids that the most important thing about diving is to keep their heads in the proper position. "If you enter the water properly," I explain, "the rest of your body will follow."

After smiling and nodding impatiently, they'd rush off to dive again, do a belly flop, and burst out of the water with grins on their faces. "Were my feet together?" they'd ask.

"I don't care if your feet are together," I replied. "Just make sure your head is straight." This scene was repeated ad nauseam over the years.

It's all about learning the basics. When I taught swimming and diving in Colorado during college, I noticed that the students who took time to learn the basics, excelled in the sport.

The Christian life is no different. If we get the basics right, the rest will follow. Jesus said, "'You shall love the Lord your God with all your heart, with all your soul, and with all your mind.' This is the first and great commandment. And the second is like it: 'You shall love your neighbor as yourself.' On these two commandments hang all the Law and the Prophets" (Matthew 22:37-40). This is as basic as it gets.

None of us know how many days we have left on our journey, but God does. The Bible tells us that He even has them numbered.

Betty, a friend and prayer partner for our first three years in Orlando, went to be with the Lord in January of 1995, just a couple of weeks before my first Passionate Hearts conference. She was my age and had children similar in age to ours, but while I enjoyed good health, she battled fallopian tube cancer–a struggle that lasted over a year. As I sat by her bedside and held her hand during some of those final hours of her life, I was forcefully reminded that regardless of the number of days God gives me, this life is transient and my time here is just a dot on the timeline of eternity. That's a sobering thought indeed.

Bertrand Russell said, "Death is the ultimate statistic. One out of one dies." Will we trust God enough to do things according to His plan until we die and finally meet Him face to face? Will we be able to hear Him say, "Well done, good and faithful servant; you were faithful over a few things, I will make you ruler over many things. Enter into the joy of your lord" (Matthew 25:21)? Have you been lulled into believing that day is an impossibly long way off?

I've been interested in biblical prophecy since I was eighteen, but in the past few years the Lord has drawn me into reading and studying the subject more than ever. I believe with all my heart that we are very close to the return of our Lord Jesus Christ, and that we will all be standing before Him soon.

As we look at our nation, there is so much for which we praise God. Many of our churches and even some towns and cities seem to be waking up spiritually. All across the nation, concerted prayer has become more widespread over the past few years as various groups call people to pray for our nation. This is a focus of Passionate Hearts, as well. Even though we are beginning to see trickles of revival here and there, we have yet to see them all come together to form a mighty river.

As we watch the news, it becomes clear, as well, that America and the world are on a course toward judgment. A war for the soul of our nation, rages daily. But the freedoms and comforts we enjoy make it easier for us to turn away from God. We live in a nation of spiritual "couch potatoes." Our strong foundation as a God-fearing nation is deteriorating. Christianity is, at times, ridiculed and often regarded as irrelevant. Many school children today have no idea what has made our nation great. We have become one of the most decadent nations on earth. We are seeing the judgment of God coming upon us. Be alert, because life will not continue to drag on as it always has. Many are so intoxicated by sex, wealth, entertainment, in our affluent society, that few take time to discern the signs of the times. This confusion in our culture will intensify as our nation collapses morally.

We have entered a new millennium that will be the most tumultuous and dangerous time in history. The Bible makes it clear that in the coming years we will see a continual increase in the shaking up of our natural world—earthquakes, tornadoes, flooding, and other natural disasters and plagues—but for now we are grateful that God is allowing us to help gather in the harvest. "The Lord is not slack concerning His promise, as some count slackness, but is longsuffering toward us, not willing that any should perish but that all should come to repentance. But the day of the Lord will come as a thief in the night" (2 Peter 3:9-10a).

So, what should we do? To begin with, we are in no position to help anyone else until we have come into a place of obedience ourselves. God cleans His own house first, and His main concern is His bride, the Church. Once you know Jesus Christ as your personal Savior, that bride includes you! When people ask me what I do, I sometimes jokingly answer that I'm a "wedding coordinator."

When God touches a land with revival, there is normally deep sorrow in the hearts of the people of God (the bride of Christ) for their sin. As we see our world in a critical need of revival and spiritual awakening, we are reminded of God's promise to Solomon concerning ancient Israel in 2 Chronicles 7:14, which can be claimed by believers of all nations. "If My people who are called by My name will humble themselves, and pray and seek My face, and turn from their wicked ways, then I will hear from heaven, and will forgive their sin and will heal their land." We must be careful not to take disobedience and sin lightly.

In February 1995, I conducted my first Passionate Hearts weekend where I watched God revive the hearts of women. That summer, our Campus Crusade for Christ conference (which included about 4,500 staff members) on the Colorado State University campus in Fort Collins, Colorado, began with a powerful message from the Lord brought by Nancy Leigh DeMoss. The floodgates of God's work seemed to fly open that summer morning as hundreds of people lined up at microphones for confession and prayer. It lasted for sixteen hours that day and continued for two more days until the conference ended.

Dr. Henry Blackaby, author of Experiencing God, also spoke at our conference. He told us how God visited Howard Payne University in Brownwood, Texas, in a similar way a few months earlier. During their Spiritual Emphasis Week, the students who were leading Bible studies and prayer on campus acknowledged that their hearts were full of sin. They fell to their knees in repentance before the Lord. Dr. Blackaby said it was like an avalanche. Students ran from the balconies and all over the auditorium. Many of them fell on their faces crying out to God before they even made it to the platform. At the end of those days together, overwhelming victory was won in the hearts of those students.

What kind of heart does God revive? The Bible repeatedly states that, "the sacrifices of God are a broken spirit, a broken and a contrite heart" (Psalm 51:17a). We will never meet God in revival until we have first met him in brokenness and humility.

Tabernacle Truth

Until we understand the seriousness of our sin problem and deal with it at the Brazen Laver of cleansing, we are not ready to enter the Holy Place or even entertain the idea of service or fellowship – with God or with others.

If we're missing the passionate presence of God in our lives, we're missing the abundance that He has promised us. "I have come that they may have life, and that they may have it more abundantly" (John 10:10b). There is nothing like cultivating intimacy to bring warmth and passion back into our relationship with Jesus Christ, which requires that we demonstrate our love by obedience. We tend to think that love if the most important thing, but love isn't even possible without humble obedience.

Jesus said, "If you love Me, keep My commandments. And I will pray the Father, and He will give you another Helper, that He may abide with you forever – the Spirit of truth" (John 14:15-17a). Notice that the immediate result of obedience is the promise of Holy Spirit power in our lives. For emphasis, this is repeated just a few verses later, "If anyone loves Me, he will keep My word; and My Father will love him, and We will come to him and make Our home with him. He who does not love Me does not keep My words" (John 14:23-24a). It is obvious that if we have an obedience problem, we have a love problem.

As we look ahead to the remaining days we have on this earth, with high expectations and hope for spiritual growth and usefulness for the Kingdom of God, the place to start is in deepening our intimacy with Jesus Christ through loving obedience.

The reward of sin is more sin and the reward of obedience is the power to obey again. We cannot rely on God's promises without obeying His commandments. Billy Graham once said, "Faith that saves has one distinguishing quality: saving faith is a faith that produces obedience; it is a faith that brings about a way of life." (John Blanchard, Gathered Gold, Darlington, England: Evangelical Press, 1984).

Points to Ponder and Pray

Are we willing to nail our colors to the mast and give God more than just a couple of hours a week, even our entire life? Read the declaration of commitment below. Can you pray through that declaration, and mean it? If so, you are on your way to an incredibly exciting, intimate, and fulfilling relationship with the God of the universe. Remember that growth is a process. Just as Rome wasn't built in a day, neither does a majestic oak tree grow from an acorn in a few months, or even years. If we are disciples of Jesus Christ, we are "in process" for all of our lives, regardless of how long or short that may be. None of us will attain perfection until we step from time into eternity, but if our heart's desire is to glorify Him with our lives, He will give us power and strength for the journey.

I Am a Disciple of Jesus Christ

I am a part of the fellowship of the unashamed. The die has been cast. I have stepped over the line. The decision has been made. I am a disciple of Jesus Christ.

I will not look back, let up, slow down, back away, or be still. My past is redeemed, my present directed, my future secure. I am finished and done with low living, sight walking, small planning, smooth knees, myopic vision, mundane talking, mediocre giving, and dwarfed goals. I no longer need preeminence, prosperity, position, promotion, or popularity. I don't have to be first, recognized, praised, regarded, or rewarded.

I now live in His presence, learn by faith, love by practice, lift by prayer, and labor in His power. My pace is set, my gait is fast, my goal is heaven. The road is narrow, the way is rough, my companions few, my guide reliable, my mission clear.

I cannot be bought, compromised, detoured, lured away, lured back, diluted, or delayed. I will not flinch in the face of sacrifice, hesitate in the presence of adversity, negotiate at the table of the enemy, ponder at the pool of popularity, or meander in the maze of mediocrity.

I won't give up, back up, let up, or hush up, till I have preached up, prayed up, paid up, stood up, and stayed up for the cause of Jesus Christ.

I am a disciple of Jesus Christ. I must go till He returns, give till it hurts, preach till I drop, tell till all know, and work till He comes. And when He comes to get His own, He'll have no problem recognizing me; my colors will be clear.

(This statement was written by a young Christian after a camp meeting and read at the May 7, 1998, National Day of Prayer. The author is unknown.)

Chapter 5

If You Think This is Beautiful, Just Wait

Terror gripped my heart as I sat in the driver's seat of my little white Chevrolet Corvair, clinging to the steering wheel and pumping my useless brake pedal. In spite of my efforts to control the car, it careened down the mile-long hill, gradually picking up speed. In the blink of an eye, it finally skidded off the road sliding sideways until it flipped over and wedged against the dirt embankment at the roadside. I don't know how many times I rolled over before my grinding dusty stop at the bottom of the hill.

I sat in the crumpled car, still clutching the steering wheel. "Thank You, Lord, and thanks, Dean," I whispered, remembering the day my good friend had insisted that he install at least one seatbelt in my car.

I tried to clear my dazed mind. All I could remember was that I'd been driving from Colorado to Arizona with Rick, a friend of my fourteen-year-old brother's. I looked at the passenger seat to see if he was all right. The seat was empty! My heart nearly stopped beating as I breathed a frantic prayer for his safety. I unbuckled my seatbelt, opened the car door, and stepped out. There on the side of the hill sat my young friend, rubbing his head, with a dazed look on his face. Not only was he alive, but he seemed to have escaped any serious physical harm. My heart leapt with gratitude.

As I sat down beside Rick on that dusty roadside, the truly important things in life stood out starkly from the trivial. I couldn't have cared less that my car was totaled or that I would never drive it again.

My mind reflected on the excitement of the previous day. It was July 4, 1969, and I had returned to my hometown of Meeker as Miss

Wool of Arizona for the annual parade and festivities. It was a magical time for me. My parents had moved to Meeker when I was in kindergarten, and it was my home until I graduated from high school in the spring of 1965.

Following the parade, my dad, trying to take good care of his "little girl," had taken my car into a local gas station to have retread tires put on the back. I wasn't more than half an hour out of town when one of those tires began to flatten.

How could I go from the grandeur of riding atop a shiny red convertible, attired in a formal gown and beautiful jeweled tiara, to a smashed little car at the bottom of a dirty ditch in less than twenty-four hours? As I sat there pondering the irony, the peace of God washed over me. Even though I was only twenty-two years old, I had learned that I was not competent to judge what God's will for my life was. My responsibility was to listen to His voice and obey. I was also beginning to learn to be content regardless of the circumstances. Only God knows everything. I do not. If I truly believed that He was the Lord of my life, then this, too, was part of His plan.

After what seemed an eternity, a highway patrol car was alerted to our plight and we were driven to the nearest town. From there I called my Dad and he came to our rescue. He dealt with the car and saw us safely onto a bus bound for Phoenix.

On that long bus ride back to Arizona, I thought a lot about God's will for my life. What would come next? I was just weeks away from joining the full-time staff of Campus Crusade for Christ, where I would spend a year touring the country with *The New Folk,* singing and sharing the Good News of Jesus Christ on college campuses. God was also solidifying in my heart and mind whom He wanted me to marry. My heart's desire was to follow His voice, *wherever* that would lead me.

And yet I wondered about God's overall plan for me. Why had He left me on earth after I came to know Him as my Savior at the age of nine? He could have easily whisked me off to heaven that very moment. Or perhaps immediately after I committed my life to Him for service at eighteen. Why did He leave me here on earth?

I had often heard the verses from the Bible that said, "For by grace you have been saved through faith, and that not of yourselves; it is the gift of God, not of works, lest anyone should boast" (Ephesians 2:8-

9). What I had never heard emphasized was the following verse: "For we are His workmanship, created in Christ Jesus for good works, which God prepared beforehand that we should walk in them."

Wow! It amazed me to think that it was all about God, and not about me after all. "You did not choose Me, but I chose you and appointed you that you should go and bear fruit, and that your fruit should remain, that whatever you ask the Father in My name He may give you" (John 15:16). I was beginning to recognize His hand in every part of my life, as I allowed His Holy Spirit to change me, empower me, and use me.

After Tip and I married in 1970, we spent two years with Campus Crusade for Christ at the University of Alabama. We shared Christ on that college campus, following up those who came to know Him as Savior, both individually and in groups. Because Tip had a degree in Physical Education, he spent most of his ministry time at Bryant Hall, the football dorm.

His love for college football, however, was and is unprecedented! Because of Tip's love for working with athletes, we moved to Tulsa, Oklahoma, in 1972 and joined the Athletes in Action weightlifting team. For the next two years we traveled ahead of the team to set up their schedule of high school and college assemblies. When we weren't on the road, Tip trained with the team at our offices in the Tulsa Athletic Club.

God provided a beautiful spot in the Tulsa countryside for us to park our mobile home. I was blissfully happy and could see nothing beyond this time and place in my life. But as I grew comfortable there, God began to speak to me about giving it all up to go overseas.

One day, as I was walking in the fields by our little lake, I was struck with the pastoral beauty of the scene. In that moment I heard God say, "If you think *this* is beautiful, just wait!"

That summer, we sold our home, our nearly new Ford Gran Torino Sport, and most of our worldly possessions to embark on God's clear call to the campuses in Ireland. After four months of cross-cultural training in California, we arrived in Ireland in January of 1975.

A few days after settling into our new home, I ventured out to explore the area. I crossed the road and began to follow a little winding path through the woods, stepping over mud puddles as I went. As I came out into an open clearing of emerald green grass and scattered trees, the panorama of the scene took my breath away. Stretching out before me was a vast yet serene river with a hauntingly beautiful old castle looming against the blue sky on the opposite bank. In that instant I was transported back to the field in Tulsa, and the words of God resonated in my ears once again.

How often do we make up our own minds about how *we* want God to use us and bless us and answer our prayers? We serve a God who loves us deeply and intimately. He longs to bless us, grow us, use us, and hear us in *His* perfect ways.

How well I remember the day in January of 1974, one year before arriving on Irish soil, when I first heard the challenge and call to overseas missions. It came in the form of a letter from some college friends, Randy and Diane McGirr, who were living in Ireland at the time. On the day their letter arrived at our office, I was at home by myself. Tip read it to me over the phone. It said, "You can count the number of trained Christians in the entire country on one hand. We are moving on to minister in Austria. Will you please come over and take our place here, and plan to stay for a minimum of six or seven years?"

The first thing that came to my mind was our comfortable lifestyle, our home, our car, and our possessions. God pierced my heart as I realized how self-centered I had become. I knelt beside our living room couch and confessed my sin in tears before the Lord. Getting up, I knew beyond a doubt that we would be going to Ireland. He had, in an instant, given me His peace.

A few months later, Tip heard that same confirmation from the Lord but through a series of interesting circumstances (including the energy crisis that hit the U.S. that year, the closing of high schools in Tulsa to Christian groups, the owner of the Tulsa Athletic Club going bankrupt, and the team being moved to California). God gave Tip a definite green light to go to a place where we could make a significant difference in the spiritual destiny of a nation's spiritually alienated university students.

During that year of planning, preparation, garage sales, packing, shipping, and intensive training, the Lord carried us in His arms. I was twenty-six years old when He called us to move to Ireland, burning our bridges behind us by getting rid of most of our earthly possessions, and twenty-seven when we landed on Irish soil. "But the Helper, the Holy Spirit, whom the Father will send in My name, He will teach you all things, and bring to your remembrance all things that I said to you. Peace I leave with you, My peace I give to you; not as the world gives do I give to you. Let not your heart be troubled, neither let it be afraid" (John 14:26-27).

As it turned out, it was not His plan for us to spend the rest of our lives there, but for almost twelve years He blessed our lives immeasurably through our obedience to that call. He grew us through the fiery furnace of many faith tests and difficult situations. He also blessed us with numerous spiritual children, grandchildren, and great-grandchildren. And He gave us four physical children as well. To Him belong all glory and honor and praise. It is *always* safe to trust the Lord!

Tabernacle Truth

If you are still counting the cost in the Outer Court and hesitant to enter the Holy Place of true service and fellowship, will you stop right here and get on your knees in humility before your Father, your Abba ("Daddy")? You do *not* want to miss His best for your life. You have no idea what you'll be missing by hanging on to what you've got. Are you willing to take that leap of faith? Can you jump off the edge into His arms and be confident that He will catch you?

It amazes me that the children of Israel had just come from horrific mind-numbing slavery in Egypt, and yet when the going got tough and they got hungry or thirsty – the first thing they wanted to do was to go back. How often we are like this. Rather than looking ahead with expectant faith, we are looking in the rear view mirror.

You don't have to be like Lot's wife; looking over your shoulder as your past goes up in flames. You, too, will turn into a figurative pillar of salt if you don't ask God to take you on to the next level in your walk with Him.

A few years ago on a trip through Tulsa, we returned to what once was our beautiful country haven in the middle of a serene cow pasture. It was difficult to locate, because it is now hidden in the midst of new roads and housing developments. As I thought back to my days of wandering those fields communing with my Lord, how grateful I was that I didn't look back.

Points to Ponder and Pray

Are you hanging onto something that you know He wants you to release? Has He given you a vision for something new?

If you trust God and stay full of hope, Satan cannot stop you. Hope is a positive expectancy of good things happening in your future. "Now faith is the substance of things hoped for, the evidence of things not seen" (Hebrews 11:1). Disobedience is the cause of a miserable life. Remember that you can do whatever you need to do. You have the strength for all things that *God* brings into your life. "I can do all things through Christ who strengthens me" (Philippians 4:13).

If you are expecting everyone to agree with you, forget it. Get ready for rejection and persecution. God promised it. Stop asking yourself how you *feel* about things; just *do* what He tells you to do. Do it now while the Spirit is flowing and don't put it off. He did not anoint you to be a quitter. He anointed you with a wonderful specific purpose in mind. Only believe and you will see the glory of God. Remember that your future is as bright as the promises of God!

Chapter 6

There's No Place Like Home

Tip and I lived in Ireland for over a decade, and rented six homes while we were there. In August of 1983, with three boys under the age of six, I became pregnant with our fourth child. We were living on the southern perimeter of Dublin, the largest city in the country. But after three long years of commuting to the college, we started praying about moving closer to the center of the city. Our ministry living allowance was not adequate to purchase a home there, so once again we began to look for a rental property.

One day, out of the blue, a friend called us from Colorado. "I've been thinking and praying about this," he said, "and I've decided I want to buy a home and ministry center for you as an investment. I have a large business deal going through any day now, and I'm expecting a large commission from it."

Of course, we were delighted and praised God for answered prayer. After months of searching, we stumbled onto the perfect place in the perfect location. When it came up for auction we phoned our friend, and he encouraged us to make a bid. We put down a 5,000-pound deposit (about $6,000), which we'd borrowed from our friendly bank manager. A few weeks later the second deposit came due. We prayed earnestly that God would provide, and just days before the payment was due, we got a call from some Irish friends who said they had some money we could borrow to put toward the second deposit. The loan amounted to 7,000 pounds—exactly what we had prayed for!

When we called our friend in Colorado to ask if we should go ahead with the second deposit, he said he had other investments he could sell if his commission didn't come through in time Feeling hopeful, we paid the second deposit.

The final amount of 68,000 Irish pounds was due just before Christmas. When nothing came from Colorado, we contacted other friends and family in the U.S. for loans. Several dear people stood with us, and we accumulated 66,000 pounds. We were certain God would bring in the extra 2,000 pounds by the end of the due date.

As the sun set that evening, we were still short 2,000 pounds. Since we could not come up with the full amount for the final payment, we had to forfeit the full deposit and the house was sold to someone else. Suddenly, we were 12,000 pounds ($13,000) *in debt,* and had no house. I was stunned. I felt nothing—no hysteria, no bitterness, just a big question mark in my mind. "Why, God? Why didn't you answer our prayers? You could have stopped this chain of events at any point along the way. We trusted You implicitly. You led us down this path, opening door after door as we prayed, only for it to all come down to this."

It took me a long time to fully understand that God is more concerned with the *process* than the *product*. When we pray, He wants our focus to be on Him and His will for our lives. As with our own parenting, His purpose is to grow us, not to see that we get everything we ask for. The biggest miracle of all was that He provided the resources, on our small living allowance, to pay off that debt.

Within a few months of losing the deposit on the house, God provided an excellent rental home in the area we were praying for, plus a Student Center/office near Trinity College (also a rental). God is never limited by the "ownership" of man. He gave us exactly what we needed, in a very different way than we expected or prayed for.

On the very day we lost our deposit, we got a call from a local petrol station telling us we had won a large Christmas basket full of goodies, including a huge turkey. Tip had submitted what they deemed the best advertising slogan at a local Texaco station: "Rudolph uses Texaco products in his sleigh, but don't tell Santa!" We smiled at God's reminder that He was still there, that He still cared, and that His promises were still valid. "I will never leave you nor forsake you" (Hebrews 13:5). When I began to fret or worry, God gently whispered in my ear that He had always provided in the past, and He didn't plan to stop now.

Over the years God has blessed us with about a dozen homes in various shapes, sizes, and locations, all of which met our needs perfectly for that particular phase of our lives. When each phase ended and He wanted us to move on, He made it abundantly clear to us, in one way or another. Each house was *our home*. It didn't matter whose name was on the deed. Owning a home is not where my security lies.

John Adams, the second president of the United States, once wrote, "I long for rural and domestic scenes, for the warbling of birds and the prattle of my children. As much as I converse with sages or heroes, they have very little of my love or admiration. I should prefer the delights of a garden to the dominion of a world." (Bob Phillips, *Phillips' Awesome Collection of Quips & Quotes,* Eugene, OR: Harvest House Publishers, 2001). No nation can be destroyed while it possesses a good home life. Travel east or west, a man's own home is still the best. This is why the saying, "There's no place like home", is so well known and used universally.

Our Lord and Savior, Jesus Christ, is right now preparing our eternal Home Sweet Home. He knows how our hearts long to be settled and secure in our own haven of rest, and so He left us with a promise. "Let not your heart be troubled; you believe in God, believe also in Me. In My Father's house are many mansions; if it were not so, I would have told you. I go to prepare a place for you. And if I go and prepare a place for you, I will come again and receive you to Myself, that where I am, there you may be also" (John 14:1-3).

God has already given me the eternal deed to my final Home, through His payment for my sins on the cross. One day soon, I will move in and never have to leave or move again.

In retrospect, it's now very clear why God did not want us to plant deep roots in Dublin. Two years after this experience He led us to return to the U.S. As I dug in my heels and resisted leaving Ireland, He got my attention on three different occasions with His words in Jeremiah 29:11-14: "For I know the thoughts that I think toward you, says the Lord, thoughts of peace and not of evil, to give you a future and a hope. Then you will call upon Me and go and pray to Me, and I will listen to you. And you will seek Me and find Me, when you search for Me with all your heart. I will be found by you, says the Lord, and I will bring you back from your captivity; I will gather you from all the nations (Ireland) and from all the places where I have driven you, says the Lord, and I will bring you to the place (U.S.) from which I cause you to be carried away captive" (parentheses mine).

There was a story in the Watchman-Examiner many years ago that says it all. "A Christian home should be Heaven begun on earth. It will be if it is the abode of warm and loving hearts. Serene but inspiring is the household which thinks, works, rejoices, and sorrows together; whose personalities are all melted down by Divine grace, uniting them in love. 'A lamp,' said Robert McCheyne, the great Scottish preacher, 'is a very small thing, and it burns calmly, and without noise, and it gives light to all that are in the house.' So there are great but quiet influences, which like the flame of a sacred lamp, fill many a home with light and fragrance. A soft, deep carpet not only diffuses a look of ample comfort, it deadens many a creaking sound; so is the peace of a Christian home. A strong curtain wards off the summer heat and the wintry wind; so a sweet family fellowship is a shield protecting all the members. A soft pillow may make some forget their misery, and a tired mind soon forgets its cares in the delights of a comfortable Christian home. Its influence is like the fresh evening breeze at the close of a burning day. There would be fewer aching hearts if there were more Christian homes. When you turn your face homeward, think of Jesus and of Heaven. Our Lord raised three persons from the dead. One was an only son; another, an only daughter; the third, an only brother. Whenever He entered a home He sanctified it with peace and radiant life. Make sure that Jesus is in the sacred presence of your home." (Walter Knight, *Knight's Master Book of New Illustrations,* Grand Rapids, MI: Eerdmans Publishing, 1956.)

After five years in Southern California, God led us to Florida, where He miraculously provided what we needed for a down payment to have our own home built. I've learned through all of our living situations that God's ultimate desire is for our hearts to be His dwelling place.

"I turned an ancient poet's book,
And found upon the page:
'Stone walls do not a prison make,
Nor iron bars a cage.'

Yes, that is true, and something more;
You'll find where'er you roam
That marble floors and gilded walls
Can never make a home.

But every house where love abides
And Friendship is a guest
Is surely home, and home, sweet home,
For there the heart can rest."
— Henry Van Dyke

Tabernacle Truth

As we return to our journey through the Tabernacle, we are now ready to move from the courtyard into the Tabernacle structure. There are two parts to this tent home: the front two-thirds is the sanctuary, or Holy Place, and the back third is the Holy of Holies. The natural light of the sun has illumined everything that we have seen to this point. That will now change as we begin to experience divine illumination and enter the realm of the Spirit in our service and fellowship. As we stand at the tent flap ready to enter, there's no looking back.

"I will abide in Your Tabernacle forever; I will trust in the shelter of Your wings" (Psalm 61:4).

Points to Ponder and Pray

When you hear the word "home", what do *you* think of? Has your heart been challenged to believe God for new things as you have read this chapter? Please take your notebook and write down all that the Holy Spirit brings to your mind. Use this as a prayer reminder in the coming months.

God welcomes you to come in. If you have obeyed the voice of God in the Outer Court, you are now invited to enter the Holy Place, the sanctuary of service and fellowship.

Chapter 7

Let There Be Light

After moving to Orlando from Southern California, I came across a paper I had written for one of my English classes when I was a senior in high school. It was one of those fortune-telling exercises English teachers love to assign. Here's what I wrote:

> According to my calculations, ten years from now I will have been married for about four years and have one child. My husband will probably be either a dentist or a doctor, since I'll be a nurse. We'll live in a very nice, modern home. I imagine I'll be working part time at the hospital, since the baby should be close to two years old. I have no idea what state we will be living in, but there is a ski slope nearby. On weekends we will probably ski in the winter, and swim and play tennis in the summer. (I've really got a rosy view dreamed up, don't I?) Our home will be either in the suburbs or in the country a ways. We will have at least two horses for riding and hunting. In order to attain all of this, I'm going to have to work pretty fast. It seems only yesterday that it was ten years ago. I was almost eight years old and in the second grade!

How accurate were my predictions? Well, by the time I was twenty-eight years old, I had been married for about four years (almost five, actually), and Tip and I did live at the edge of town near the country. But that's where the similarity ended. We had just arrived in Ireland to begin a twelve–year stint as campus missionaries. We had no children, there were no mountains or snow, and the closest I ever got to a hospital was when I had a baby two years later.

We all have dreams for our lives, and yet they often bear little resemblance to the reality we experience. God emphasizes His supremacy in Isaiah 55:8-9:

> For My thoughts are not your thoughts,
> Nor are your ways My ways," says the Lord.
> "For as the heavens are higher than the earth,
> So are My ways higher than your ways,
> And My thoughts than your thoughts.

Just four months after I wrote that high school paper, my life turned around 180 degrees at a Bible camp in the mountains of Colorado. Instead of entering the University of Colorado that fall to study nursing, I ended up at Grand Rapids School of the Bible and Music in Michigan. This was followed by a year at Biola University in California and two years at Arizona State University before I joined the staff of Campus Crusade for Christ to sing with *The New Folk*.

I began to see life differently one Friday in July in 1965, when God put a dream in my heart to love and serve Him, the King of the universe. The peace that swept over me was incredible. My week at Twin Peaks Bible Camp in the mountains of Colorado was coming to a close, and as I sat on my bunk considering everything I'd heard that week, I made a conscious decision to cease my endless rationalizing and go *His* way instead of my own. I sensed a weight lifting from me, like slipping off a heavy backpack. I felt like I could have floated right up to the ceiling just by untying my tennis shoes. There was no doubt in my mind—something major had happened to me. I was no longer the same person.

I have desired to follow the Lord with all my heart from that point on. But spiritual growth is an ongoing journey, not a destination. After more than thirty years, I still struggle daily against my three worst enemies: the world, the flesh, and the devil. I still live in a dark and sinful world system that I rub up against constantly. It dirties me and requires continual cleansing. The temptations and desires of the flesh are always tugging at me to drift away from my first love. And

Satan and his cohorts hate me enough to actively orchestrate attacks and wage war against me.

The realities of life seem hollow in comparison to what I expected when I was dreaming in high school. This is why my passion must be single. I must daily choose to loosen my grip on earthly things, even the people I love most, and keep my focus on the One who died for me.

Just as Lazarus had to remove his grave clothes after Jesus raised him from the dead, we are responsible to "work out your own salvation with fear and trembling; for it is God who works in you both to will and to do for His good pleasure. Do all things without complaining and disputing, that you may become blameless and harmless, children of God without fault in the midst of a crooked and perverse generation, among whom you shine as lights in the world, holding fast the word of life, so that I may rejoice in the day of Christ that I have not run in vain or labored in vain" (Philippians 2:12b-16).

To accomplish the purity in our lives that God desires, we have to make sure we don't allow the tentacles of sin to wrap themselves around our ankles and trip us up. It must be our daily choice to walk in freedom, rather than remain in bondage. Only then can we live in power and victory so God can bless us and use us for His glory. That's why He left us here on earth after we trusted Him as Savior, after all.

Nothing has changed since the first man and woman were placed on this earth. The lust of the flesh, the lust of the eyes, and the pride of life determine how most of us live our lives. Rather than being thermostats and setting the temperature around us, we are thermometers who simply register the existing temperature. Instead of setting the pace in the race, we follow the pace car. Jesus Christ said to his disciples, "Follow Me, and I will make you fishers of men. They *immediately left ... and followed Him*" (Matthew 4:19b-20, emphasis mine).

Tabernacle Truth

We have entered the gate to the Outer Court. Our sins have been forgiven by the blood of Jesus Christ at the altar of sacrifice (salvation). We have confessed all sin in our lives and been washed at the Brazen Laver of cleansing (sanctification). Now we are ready to enter the sanctuary, the Holy Place. This is the center of service and fellowship in the Tabernacle.

The first thing our eyes are drawn to is the lamp stand, the light, because it is the only means for seeing evidence of God in His Holy Place. It has a single shaft with three branches proceeding from each side, for a total of seven lamp stands. (Seven is the number of perfection and completion in God's Word.) Of these seven, one stands by itself. The Spirit of the Lord is the center shaft that proceeds directly from the "root" of the lamp stand (Isaiah 11:1-2). The other six represent wisdom, understanding, counsel, might, knowledge, and fear. God will develop these attributes in our lives as we allow Him to live His life in and through us.

Jesus prayed for all believers in John 17 when He said "that they all may be one, as You, Father, are in Me, and I in You; that they also may be one in Us, that the world may believe that You sent Me. And the glory which You gave Me I have given them, that they may be one just as We are one: I in them, and You in Me; that they may be made perfect in one, and that the world may know that You have sent Me, and have loved them as You have loved Me" (21-23). It would be hard to describe our oneness and unity in Christ more succinctly than that! It is a conscious decision, minute by minute, to tap into the Life Source that comes through the root to the branches. As we do that, it is His responsibility to produce fruit in our lives.

The gifts of the Spirit, which God gives every believer at salvation, represent Christ's *ministry*. These are described in First Corinthians 12:4-7, 11-12.

> There are diversities of gifts, but the same Spirit. There are differences of ministries, but the same Lord. And there are diversities of activities, but it is the same God who works all in all. But the manifestation of the Spirit is given to each one for the profit of all ... But one and the same Spirit works all these things, distributing to each one individually as He wills. For as the body is one and has many members, but all the members of that one body, being many, are one body, so also is Christ.

The fruit of the Spirit represent Christ's *personality*. When we are connected to the root and the Holy Spirit is allowed to flow through our lives, His personality takes over. "But the fruit of the Spirit is love, joy, peace, longsuffering, kindness, goodness, faithfulness, gentleness, self-control. … And those who are Christ's have crucified the flesh with its passions and desires. If we live in the Spirit, let us also walk in the Spirit" (Galatians 5:22-25).

We could save ourselves a lot of agonizing prayer for more love, joy, peace, patience, kindness, goodness, faith, gentleness, and self-control by simply focusing on being filled with the Holy Spirit and drawing on His power. We need only to pray, "Lord, cleanse my heart and make me a pure and useable container where You can live. Fill me with Your precious Holy Spirit, and may it be in abundance so that it will overflow into the lives of others." He produces the fruit in us. It's not about us, but Him. The gospel of John begins with this truth.

> In the beginning was the Word, and the Word was with God, and the Word was God. He was in the beginning with God. All things were made through Him, and without Him nothing was made that was made. In Him was life, and the life was the light of men (1:1-4).

In the Sermon on the Mount, Jesus said, "I am the light of the world. He who follows Me shall not walk in darkness, but have the light of life" (John 8:12). He went on to say that, "*You* are the light of the world. Let *your* light so shine before men, that they may see *your* good works and glorify *your* Father in heaven" (Matthew 5:14a, 16). He has passed the baton on to us. The Apostle Paul emphasizes this truth when he writes:

> For you were once darkness, but now you are light in the Lord. Walk as children of light (for the fruit of the Spirit is in all goodness, righteousness, and truth), finding out what is acceptable to the Lord. And have no fellowship with the unfruitful works of darkness, but rather expose them. But all things that are exposed are made manifest by the light, for whatever makes manifest is light (Ephesians 5:8-11, 13).

Those who walk in purity and obedience are children of light.

We are the light that must be kept burning so others can see His presence. This reminds me of the old children's song that talks about letting "this little light of mine" shine. When we hide our light, those who walk in darkness will have a difficult time seeing the light of God. After all, we are the heavenly lamp stands of this age, meant to reflect Jesus to a dark world.

The brightness of our light depends on how much oil (a symbol of the Holy Spirit) we allow Christ to pour on us and into us continually. The Spirit of God is our fuel to shine, and being filled (or fueled) is a continual process. We are commanded to be filled with the Spirit in Ephesians 5:18. In this verse, the verb *filled* is a continuing action verb: "be (being) filled with the Spirit." If we allow that light to burn brightly, we are filled with the Holy Spirit. And when we are filled with the Spirit, another chain reaction takes place. We find ourselves producing the fruit of the Spirit.

Lamps do not talk; they illuminate. Lighthouses make no noise; they give light. Our walk as a Christian must be a living sermon.

The Light
A tender child of summers three,
Seeking her little bed at night,
Paused on the dark stair timidly,
"Oh, Mother, take my hand," said she,
And then the dark will all be light."

We older children grope our way,
From dark behind to dark before;
And only when our hands we lay,
Dear Lord, in Thine, the night is day,
And there is darkness nevermore.

Reach downward to the sunless days
Wherein our guides are blind as well,
And faith is small and hope delays;
Take Thou the hands of prayer we raise,
And let us feel the light of Thee.
—John Greenleaf Whittier

Points to Ponder and Pray

"God is light and in Him is no darkness at all. If we say that we have fellowship with Him, and walk in darkness, we lie and do not practice the truth. But if we walk in the light as He is in the light, we have fellowship with one another, and the blood of Jesus Christ His Son cleanses us from all sin. If we say that we have no sin, we deceive ourselves, and the truth is not in us. If we confess our sins, He is faithful and just to forgive us our sins and to cleanse us from all unrighteousness" (1 John 1:5b-9).

Please take a brief interlude to listen and respond to the still, small voice of God. Are you hiding your light, or are you putting it on a lamp stand for all to see? Is it giving light to all who are in your house? Are you letting your light shine so that others may see your good works and glorify your Father in heaven? Is there sin in your life that you need to confess?

What specific things will you jot down and begin to work on today that will move you out of the shadows and into the light? Remember that this is a lifelong journey, not a destination. It is a minute-by-minute decision to walk in the light.

God's first recorded words in Genesis were, "Let there be light" (1:3). Hear Him whisper those words to you every morning when you open your eyes. "Today, My child, let there be light."

"Come and let us walk in the light of the Lord" (Isaiah 2:5).

Chapter 8

More Gratitude, Less Attitude

"What do you mean, Josh left his bike out last night and it's gone?" How many of our bikes had been lost, stolen, or run over by construction vehicles? Frankly, I'd lost count. Fuming through the kitchen, I slammed every cupboard door, making wild threats about leaving Ireland if one more thing of value to me was stolen, crashed, absorbed by a real estate agent, or torn apart by a dog. "Leave me alone, God," I shouted at the ceiling. "I've had enough."

Wondering what had just snapped in his wife, my brave husband stood peering at me from the kitchen door. I turned on my heel and stormed out of the room, giving the door a solid kick as I left. As I stomped into the living room, slamming the door behind me, the tears erupted. I couldn't understand why such a trivial episode was putting my sanity to the test. Hadn't I come through much tougher circumstances relatively unscathed?

A bike was nothing compared to cars. Shortly before we moved to Ireland, my older brother, Gary, had graciously given us his VW Beetle. We drove the tiny red bug for years, but after our three children came along, it was a day of great celebrating when we replaced it with a station wagon.

The same week we finished paying off the loans for the deposit on the house we'd lost, God put me through another test of how well I could loosen my grip on material possessions. As I was driving Josh to preschool, a motorcycle tried to pass me at an intersection and hit me full tilt, throwing himself and his bike all over the road. After determining that the motorcyclist was unharmed, my initial response was, "So what's a dented car to the God of the universe?" The repair bill was just pocket change in comparison to the house debt.

Before the station wagon even found its way to the garage for repairs, an ashen-faced neighbor boy came to our door and said, "Come quickly. Josh has been badly hurt." With baby Trinity in my arms and six-year-old Jason close at my heels, I raced to the neighbor's house. I found my three-year-old son saturated in blood and screaming hysterically. The neighbor's dog, a black Labrador, had attacked him. Josh's eye was swollen shut, the size of a golf ball, and he had sustained a deep gash across his eyelid. I wondered if he'd been permanently blinded. His scalp was ripped open, exposing his skull from one ear all the way to the top of his head and halfway down the other side. Was his skull fractured? Would he grow up with brain damage?

I wrapped him in a bath towel and cradled him in my arms as my neighbor drove us to the hospital, swearing at the rush-hour traffic in frustration. I prayed softly in Josh's ear and he grew calm. But I was far from calm.

How could God allow this to happen? I had prayed with the boys that very morning for physical safety and protection from harm. Why had God not answered my prayer?

Why did I park near the neighbor's back gate when I brought the boys home from school? Why didn't I bring Josh in the house with me instead of letting him go play with his friends in that yard? Why hadn't the dog attacked the boy who had been pestering him with a squirt gun instead of my son?

After expressing my confusion to God as honestly as possible, I realized that dwelling on the *whys* and *what-ifs* never does a bit of good. We seldom get an answer that fully satisfies. "Therefore humble yourselves under the mighty hand of God, that He may exalt you in due time, casting all your care upon Him, for He cares for you" (1 Peter 4:6-7). We are given the same admonition in Psalm 55:22. "Cast your burden on the Lord, And He shall sustain you; He shall never permit the righteous to be moved."

The Lord flooded my mind with many Scriptures that I knew from the past. It was one of those times when I was so grateful that I had tucked them away in my heart for future reference. Even though I don't know when I will need them, God does.

> Fear not, for I am with you;
> Be not dismayed, for I am your God.
> I will strengthen you,
> Yes, I will help you,
> I will uphold you with My righteous right hand (Isaiah 41:10).

A couple of chapters later we receive another powerful promise from God.

> Fear not, for I have redeemed you;
> I have called you by your name;
> You are Mine.
> When you pass through the waters, I will be with you;
> And through the rivers, they shall not overflow you.
> When you walk through the fire, you shall not be burned,
> Nor shall the flame scorch you.
> For I am the Lord your God (Isaiah 43:1b-3a).

As I endured that infinitely long car ride to the hospital, holding my precious hurting bundle in my arms, I realized I had to believe the God who made that promise in Isaiah. Worrying and fretting only reveals unbelief, which is sin. I needed to be honest, of course, but I also needed to cling to Him. I had to believe that He was in control of every situation, including this one, and that His promise in Romans was written for me, and for Josh: "All things work together for good to those who love God, to those who are the called according to His purpose" (8:28).

That day, I began to learn in a deeper way than ever before that it is not the trials in life that defeat me, but my attitude toward them. I can choose to view trials as a hammer to destroy me, or as God's chisel to fashion my life. We are reminded in the book of James to "count it all joy when you fall into various trials, knowing that the testing of your faith produces patience. But let patience have its perfect work, that you may be perfect and complete, lacking nothing" (1:2-4).

The other truth that rang loudly in my ears and heart was the necessity of giving thanks. This is the true proof of our belief in God.

I can lament over a large amount of money being wasted on a house deposit and the shallow promises of a friend, or I can thank God for providing the money to satisfy the debt, not to mention the valuable lessons learned through the situation. I can gripe about my crashed car, or I can thank God because no one was badly hurt in the accident. I can complain about the theft of our personal property, or I can thank God that the break-in happened without injury to us. I can bemoan Josh's injuries and waste precious time thinking of ways to get even with our neighbors and their dog, or I can thank God for sparing Josh's eyesight, his brain, and his life, letting God deal with the neighbors and their dog. I can grieve over the year that Josh experienced double vision, or I can thank God for guiding us to a surgeon who was able to correct it.

My attention must be diverted from the pain in my life, be it small or large, and placed on the One who loves me and has a wonderful plan for my life. As Corrie ten Boom said, "God has no problems, only plans." Life is full of things we can't do anything about, but which we are supposed to do something *with*. No matter what difficulties come into my life, I am told, "in everything give thanks; for this is the will of God in Christ Jesus for you" (1 Thessalonians 5:18). God doesn't let up until we have internalized this lesson: be thankful in everything, wherever, with whomever—all the time!

When I pour out my heart to the Lord, sharing with Him all my fears, frustrations, irritations, complaints, hurts, He understands ... and He can do something about it. More gratitude, less attitude!

There is a lot of pain in families, and most of it isn't physical pain. Some people seem to have perfect families, but ours certainly isn't. I doubt that yours is either. Is it possible to have a family where everyone loves each other at the same time? In reality I find that there is often a sorrow in most families where one member at any given time is angry, self-absorbed or hurt, demanding or needing more attention and robbing others in the process. It's the person who cuts with anger, divides with rebellion, wounds with words. And the whole family bleeds.

Is it part of the function of a family to be wounded and bruised for another's sake? And when is it too much? It would be wonderful if life was a rose garden without thorns, but real families have scars. They contain people who are willful and confused for a short time or for a lifetime. There's always someone who wishes another one was different or one who is unwilling to extend the grace and forgiveness that they themselves have received. Someone hurt another's feelings and he or she isn't sorry. Families are imperfect like life is imperfect. The imperfections and unique characteristics are a part of every family.

Jesus is my perfect example to follow. He showed me by His life how there is unity through humility. I am not very good at that, but I know that He is working in me. The good news is that He promised that He will not give up on me. "...being confident of this very thing, that He who has begun a good work in you will complete it until the day of Jesus Christ" (Philippians 1:6). "...fulfill my joy by being like-minded, having the same love, being of one accord, of one mind. Let nothing be done through selfish ambition or conceit, but in lowliness of mind let each esteem others better than himself. Let each of you look out not only for his own interests, but also for the interests of others" (Philippians 2:2-4).

I am like everyone else in the human race – the walking wounded, imperfect, but still in the race, seeing each new day with the potential for healing, sunshine, growth, His comforting presence – and perhaps tomorrow more rain.

The sorrows and the incompleteness have a purpose. They help make me who I am. The added weight brings strength to sagging muscles. I have to trust that God is in control each and every day, and that I am His child. I am compelled to live out the reality that "My grace is sufficient for you, for My strength is made perfect in weakness" (2 Corinthians 12:9). And perhaps what I am and who I am can help feed another hungry soul. "God of all comfort, who comforts us in all our tribulation, that we may be able to comfort those who are in any trouble, with the comfort with which we ourselves are comforted by God" (2 Corinthians 1:3-4).

As I reflected on Josh's stolen bike, my outburst, and what God had shown me, my rage began to lose momentum. Then my husband appeared at the door trying to stifle a smile. He said, "One of our neighbors saw Josh's bike outside just before dark last night. He put it into his shed for safekeeping."

I had the distinct impression that God was giggling at my misreading of the situation. The Everlasting Father of the Universe cared enough to bend close to me and not be offended by my presumptuous temper tantrum. How could He love me so? I had behaved badly. And yet, it seems He often touches my life most when I am at my worst.

Thus, on one angry morning in my life, I once again came to terms with the One who knows all about me and loves and accepts me anyway. Even though He was not pleased with my behavior, blessings were poured out on me and I was changed because of His grace.

Tabernacle Truth

The Scriptures are filled with admonitions to praise God and to give thanks in everything. They are also filled with warnings against the flip side of this, which is our propensity to be fearful, to complain, and to perpetuate strife and anger. As we prepare to enter the Holy Place, we must examine our hearts. In Psalm 100 God makes it vividly clear how we are to enter His gates. If you know the chorus that was written to fit these words, sing this to the Lord right now.

> Make a joyful shout to the Lord, all you lands!
> Serve the Lord with gladness;
> Come before His presence with singing.
> Know that the Lord, He is God;
> It is He who has made us, and not we ourselves;
> We are His people and the sheep of His pasture.
>
> Enter into His gates with thanksgiving,
> And into His courts with praise.
> Be thankful to Him, and bless His name.
> For the Lord is good;
> His mercy is everlasting,
> And His truth endures to all generations.

Points to Ponder and Pray

Have you experienced God's undeserved grace and favor in your life? If you're anything like me, you receive it on a daily basis. Why not stop for a moment right now to thank Him? While you're at it, ask Him to help you develop an "attitude of gratitude."

Fear and anger are two of the strongest emotions that we experience as human beings. Often the anger is just an emotional release for a fear that lies beneath it.

As you think about anger, keep in mind that the Word of God admonishes us to "be swift to hear, slow to speak, slow to wrath; for the wrath of man does not produce the righteousness of God" (James 1:19b-20). Solomon, the wisest man who ever lived, gives us very wise advice in Proverbs 16:32.

He who is slow to anger is better than the mighty,
And he who rules his spirit than he who takes a city.

When you feel anger rising up within you, follow these steps to victory:

1) Admit that you're angry and "own it".
2) Identify where it is coming from.
3) Confess your sin of fear and unbelief.
4) Deal with it quickly.
"Be angry, and do not sin: do not let the sun go down on your wrath, nor give place to the devil" (Ephesians 4:26-27).
5) Choose to forgive immediately. (It is a choice, not a feeling.)
"Pursue peace with all people, and holiness, without which no one will see the Lord: looking carefully lest anyone fall short of the grace of God; lest any root of bitterness springing up cause trouble, and by this many become defiled" (Hebrews 12:14-15).
6) Continue to walk in love and kindness by faith.
7) Thank God for His undeserved grace and favor in your life.

Chapter 9

Food for Life

"What on earth is a sherry trifle?" During our first Christmas in Ireland, David and Pam Wilson, our Irish director and his wife, graciously invited us to Christmas dinner. I offered to bring something to contribute to the meal, and Pam asked me to bring, of all things, *sherry trifle*! Feeling confident that I could handle this challenge, I went out and bought an Irish cookbook. The day before Christmas, I studied the trifle recipe and carefully prepared what I hoped would be an Irish delight for all.

As dessert was served on that evening, everyone plunged in with eager anticipation. As the first forkful made its way into each person's mouth, everyone seemed to stop chewing simultaneously. I, too, found it rather strong, but I'd never *had* trifle before.

Pam looked at me with a quizzical expression. "Just how much sherry did you put into this trifle, Laurie?"

I assured her that I had followed the recipe to the letter. "It called for a glassful, so that's what I put in." Immediately, everyone at the table dropped their sour expressions and burst out in uproarious laughter! To Americans, a glass is a tumbler. To the Irish, a glass is a small shot glass.

I apologized profusely for ruining the dessert, but no one was upset. If anyone had lit a match, I'm sure the entire dining room would have gone up in flames. The most humorous part of the day was watching our Irish director's father, a godly Plymouth Brethren gentleman, almost single-handedly finish off the entire trifle.

People the world over love to eat. One of the biggest businesses in the new millennium is weight control. We think and talk constantly about our favorite foods, snacks, meals, and restaurants. Fast food has become a reality in many people's lives. Unfortunately, this is true both physically and spiritually.

Tabernacle Truth

As we come into the Holy Place of the Tabernacle and the tent flap closes behind us, we are enveloped in total darkness, with the exception of a single object on our left—the Lampstand. As we glance to our right, we see what the beautiful light is illuminating. Food! The Table of Shewbread (pronounced 'show-bred') was a place of communion and fellowship. It contained food (the Bread of the Presence) and was a center of fellowship, much like mealtime is today.

Psychologists have observed that one of the greatest losses of communication within modern families is the rarity of gathering around the table for a family meal. We can't begin to estimate the far-reaching effects on the family, the church, and our nation, of trading that time of family unity for other activities. It is now common knowledge that one of the most determinative factors in the growth of children toward success and achievement is a daily family meal.

I admit that baking a good loaf of bread these days is much simpler than it was for my grandmother. I just dump the ingredients into my bread machine before I go to bed and—presto!—a lovely loaf of fresh bread is waiting for me when I get up in the morning.

To nourish others spiritually, we must go through the same process. We often try to wiggle out of the "sifting" and the "hot ovens" that come our way in the Christian life. And yet, God not only allows such times, but He actually orchestrates them for our developmental growth as well as the resulting effect to others. "Blessed be the God and Father of our Lord Jesus Christ, the Father of mercies and God of all comfort, who comforts us in all our tribulation, that we may be able to comfort those who are in any trouble, with the comfort with which we ourselves are comforted by God. For as the sufferings of Christ abound in us, so our consolation also abounds through Christ" (2 Corinthians 1:3-5).

We begin with a simple grain of wheat, which is a symbol of our life. "Unless a grain of wheat falls into the ground and dies, it remains alone; but if it dies, it produces much grain. He who loves his life will lose it, and he who hates his life in this world will keep it for eternal life " (John 12:24-25). As we begin to live for Christ and die to our own desires, we find that God produces a great harvest of wheat through that one grain that was buried in the ground and died.

As we mix the water of the Word ["that He might sanctify and cleanse her with the washing of water by the word" (Ephesians 5:26)] with the "sifted flour" that results from the pulverizing of our wheat harvest, we add the oil as we live by faith in the power of the Holy Spirit. The parable of the wise and foolish virgins in Matthew 25:1-13 is an excellent example of the eternal importance of the oil. The only ingredient left to include is the salt for flavor. We, as believers in Jesus Christ, are "the salt of the earth" (Matthew 5:13a). The final step is the hot oven, which brings out the flavor and makes it appetizing for consumption. This process results in nourishment, strength, and growth. None of us relish the "hot ovens" in our lives, and yet that's a vital step in becoming useful and useable for God.

Every part of the Tabernacle is a picture of our Lord Jesus Christ. "For the bread of God is He who comes down from heaven and gives life to the world. … And Jesus said to them, 'I am the bread of life. He who comes to Me shall never hunger, and he who believes in Me shall never thirst'" (John 6:33, 35). God showed His glory as *the bread of heaven.* The most basic fundamental of our faith is the cross of Jesus Christ. His body was broken for us. If we ever stray from the bedrock of our Lord's sacrificial death, we may sound interesting or entertaining, but we will never have power in our lives.

In our world today, the cross on which Jesus died carries about as much weight as the tiny replica people wear on chains around their neck. However, from God's point of view, it is of more importance than all the empires of the world. In our affluent, consumer-oriented society, the cross is not good news at all. We want a comfortable Christianity, but that was never God's intention.

When we talk about the cross, the energy of God is released. As we sense God urging us to give up the struggle to run our own lives, and we say, "Here am I! Send me" (Isaiah 6:8b), we willingly become broken bread and poured-out wine for others. We may want to choose the particulars of our own problems and trials, but it doesn't work that way. When God uses someone we dislike, or some set of circumstances we would never choose, to cause us to trust Him and grow, we resist. But to bake a delicious loaf of bread, the wheat must first be crushed, and then heated by fire.

Jesus promised that if we follow Him, we too will experience suffering. "A servant is not greater than his master. If they persecuted Me, they will also persecute you (John 15:20a). Our attention must not be fixed on the pain in our lives but on the One who loves us and offers a wonderful plan for our lives.

When my first pregnancy ended in miscarriage after six years of marriage, I was devastated. But God said, "Laurie, trust Me."

When I went into the hospital in Ireland to have a simple mole removed and I woke up from anesthesia to find twenty-one big black stitches in my face, He said, "Laurie, trust Me!"

During the cold, dark winter of 1981, when I had three sons under the age of four and I experienced months of postnatal depression in a freezing house with no heat but a fireplace, He said, "Laurie, *trust* Me!"

When I felt that my ministry was all in the past and I could see no future, He said, "Laurie, trust Me!"

When God said, "You must leave Ireland, your time here is over," and I grieved over the loss of my adopted homeland, He said, "Laurie, trust Me!"

Whenever I choose to walk away from Him rather than follow Him, He says over and over again, "Laurie, trust Me!"

What is God saying to you today in your trials, your pain, your fears, your losses, your wrong choices? He tells you the same thing He has told me again and again–to trust Him completely. Are you discouraged by where you are financially, spiritually, emotionally, or physically? Do you feel like you can't get all the problems solved in your own home, much less in another person's life, certainly not in the world? I understand. I have felt this way many times. Even in these difficult times there are joys and lessons to be learned if we just listen to the still small voice of God. Regardless of where we are in our lives, there are greater things ahead for every one of us. But we must be patient and content with where He has us right now and commit *every* concern to Him in prayer.

Our lives are made up of seasons. The one you are in right now will not last forever. But what you *do* in this season will determine what your future holds as you walk in your pain and trials, and allow Him to have His way. He wants us to bring our requests to Him with hearts that trust Him, regardless of whether His answers to our prayers are *yes, no,* or *wait.*

Over my years of walking hand in hand with the Lord, I've experienced jubilant springs, fruitful summers, barren autumns, and the crushing defeat of depressing winters. The book of Proverbs is jam packed with the wisdom of God through Solomon to help me through every season I encounter, but this is one of my favorite passages.

> "Trust in the Lord with all your heart,
> And lean not on your own understanding;
> In all your ways acknowledge Him
> And He shall direct your paths" (3:5-6).

Once the bread has been baked in that hot oven, the sweet aroma wafts out. As it is sliced and served, it becomes delicious nourishment to others. One of my favorite memories from childhood is waiting for a fresh loaf of bread to be taken from the oven in my grandmother's kitchen on her farm in North Dakota. While it was still warm, I would slather it with freshly churned butter and homemade strawberry jam. Is your mouth watering yet?

Do you find the bread of Christ's presence as enticing as what I just described? We build our relationships with Him through habitual encounters, by allowing Him to speak to us through His words found in the Bible. "Your words were found, and I ate them, and Your word was to me the joy and rejoicing of my heart; for I am called by Your name" (Jeremiah 15:16). As you feed your faith, your doubts will starve to death.

To be broken bread in His hands, we must live in obedience and let Him do what He chooses in our lives. There is no greater satisfaction and fulfillment in life than to allow Him to produce the kind of bread and wine that will benefit countless others because we chose to walk with Him. May God not find the *whine* in us as He allows the crushing of the wheat and the grapes in our lives. Let's allow the aging process to produce the best and the sweetest wine, rather than vinegar. He will give us the grace to face anything He brings our way. Sorrow looks back, worry looks around, but faith looks up.

Remember that God wants spiritual fruit, not religious nuts. The mighty oak tree was once a little nut that held its ground. You can grow a weed overnight, but not an oak tree. The size and strength of the mighty oak is in direct proportion to the time spent growing. Do not despair in how far you have to go and what you lack, but rather rejoice in the time and opportunity that God is giving you to grow and be used to further His Kingdom on earth.

Our only aim in life must be that the Son of God is glorified, which means we need to stop telling Him what to do. Unless we can create the entire universe in six days, then perhaps giving advice to God isn't such a good idea! When we wander away from God, everyone around us will suffer. As we deepen our intimacy with Him and submit to His will, only then are we able to feed and nourish others.

I have learned how to make an excellent sherry trifle, and I am continuing to learn daily how to nourish others by breaking the Bread of life to feed the hungry.

Points to Ponder and Pray

Please stop for a few minutes to answer three of life's most important questions. Jot down ideas the Spirit gives you to make developmental changes in these areas. Once you have completed your list, use it as your prayer list in the coming months.

1) Am I self-centered or Savior-centered?
2) Am I seeking comfort or character?
3) Am I concerned with getting or giving?

Chapter 10

Gatekeepers

Susannah Wesley is one of my heroes. She was an amazing woman in the 1800's who was an awesome woman of God and an incredible mother. She was vigilant in recognizing worldly influences, even in the ordinary everyday matters of life. She was determined to serve the Lord faithfully in the area where He had given her responsibility, which was her home. She gave birth to nineteen children in nineteen years. Nine died in infancy, and she home schooled the ten who lived. She personally taught them reading, writing, math, Bible, and the Christian disciplines.

Susannah started a Bible study in her home, and her practical teaching soon attracted some 200 people to attend. That was not considered a proper thing for a woman to do in that day and age, but she didn't care whether others approved of her or not, as long as she felt she was following the voice of God.

Her example and modeling were even more important than her instruction. Susannah's godliness made her children continually aware of God's demand for obedience and purity. She believed that the crux of religion is nothing more than doing God's will rather than following our own.

She ran a very tight ship, one that would seem downright rigid by today's standards, but her children learned the disciplines from her that would become a part of the fiber of their lives. During every hour of the day they had a specific regimen of what they were to do, including private prayer, Bible study, public prayers, etc. It was a hectic schedule, but through such disciplines she raised two young men whose adult ministry brought a breath of new life and revival to England and beyond. Those sons, John and Charles Wesley, lit a spiritual fire that leaped oceans and within a few years had encircled the globe. They were the founders of the Methodist movement, which was named for the carefully methodical approach to the spiritual life they learned as children at their mother's knee.

Because of her model of consistency in obeying God's will, even in the little things, a revival of personal holiness began within her family and eventually spread throughout the world. Even after death, her influence continued to burn within the hearts of her sons. Charles wrote hymns until he was past eighty and John continued his ministry into his eighty-seventh year. Had his mother been alive, she would have rejoiced in knowing that the tiny flame she and her husband had lit was still burning.

As we think about the impact that we desire to have on others, especially our husband, children, and grandchildren, Proverbs 31:10-31 summarizes what a virtuous wife should be like. This section of Scripture concludes with,

> "Charm is deceitful and beauty is passing,
> But a woman who fears the Lord, she shall be praised.
> Give her of the fruit of her hands,
> And let her own works praise her in the gates."

We need to live in purity for the Lord, for ourselves, for our families, and for the world, keeping in mind that God has given us a tremendous responsibility. The Scriptures warn us that in the last days there will be people who are "lovers of themselves, lovers of money, boasters, proud, blasphemers, disobedient to parents, unthankful, unholy, unloving, unforgiving, slanderers, without self-control, brutal, despisers of good, traitors, headstrong, haughty, lovers of pleasure rather than lovers of God, having a form of godliness but denying its power. *And from such people turn away! For of this sort are those who creep into households and make captives of gullible women loaded down with sins, led away by various lusts, always learning and never able to come to the knowledge of the truth"* (2 Timothy 3:1-7, emphasis mine).

Think for a minute about all of the ungodly programming and outright lies that are available to us through television, videos, radio,

CDs, computers, etc. Though we may pride ourselves in not inviting cult members into our homes, we invite other sinister guests in through the technology in our homes without thinking twice about it. The present survey by Barna Research indicates that the average American spends about three-and-a-half hours watching television daily. How would you rank yourself on the "worldly influence" chart? I personally enjoy unwinding at night with news shows or old clean sitcoms, but I have to be continually watchful, not only about *what* goes into my mind, but *how much*.

We determined when our children were small that TV is an enemy of godliness, and that it was not going to replace our family meal or their daily time with God. We had no television when the children were small, and when we *did* get one, we kept it under "lock and key"—literally!

Once our kids entered high school, we gave them more freedom with their personal decisions concerning music, TV, and movies, and they are learning how to make wise choices. This is something I still pray about, even though their age range is now seventeen to twenty-four years old.

My parents were schoolteachers, and they decided that my brothers and I would not grow up with a TV, so I didn't watch television until I was in my late thirties. Did I miss it? Not for a minute. I loved the outdoors, swimming, skiing, sledding, ice skating, biking, hunting, picnics, fishing, horseback riding, reading, music, dancing, cheerleading, hanging out with my friends, drama, and music. I was in every club in high school except Future Farmers of America!

Whenever our children asked to see or do something, we based our decision on the scriptural standard of Philippians 4:8. "Whatever things are true, whatever things are noble, whatever things are just, whatever things are pure, whatever things are lovely, whatever things are of good report, if there is any virtue and if there is anything praiseworthy—meditate on these things."

If you find television is hard to avoid when it's sitting there in front of you, like having chocolate on the counter and trying not to eat it, then by all means move it!

Music choices are just as important as television and movies. We moms must be "watchmen on the walls" in these areas. As our children's music goes, so go their minds, spirits, thought life, and behavior. Feed them good Christian, age-related music from the time they're toddlers. I had to work at this, copying old children's records onto tapes when we lived overseas, then eventually changing over to CDs. This is one of my primary gifts I give my children. It really helped turn our sons away from secular rock, rap, and heavy metal when they were young teens.

The same vigilance is required with video and computer games. Don't be lulled into thinking, "Oh, what's the harm in it?" Sometimes we have to be the bad guy, monitoring closely what we allow in our homes. Your children may not appear grateful when you step in to lead or guide them, but someday they will come back to thank you.

Most parents don't realize that the types of books and toys their children play with can have an adverse effect on them. When our daughters were younger, they knew that books on ghosts or witches were not allowed, and R.L. Stine's *Goosebumps* series was off-limits. The latest craze is Harry Potter books, which we have a responsibility to read so we can make an informed decision as to whether or not we want our children to read them. In my opinion, this is the kind of soft-core stuff that makes our children more comfortable with the occult as they get older.

The *Babysitter's Club* books became an issue when our daughter Trinity, who is an avid reader, became addicted to them in elementary school. She began slipping into a fantasy world, and she started experiencing difficulty concentrating in class. I had to remove these books from her life, because an addiction is not something you can dabble in. These particular books seem fairly innocuous, but again, it opens the door to an obsession with trashy romance novels.

What about Barbie dolls? Yes, my girls received them from friends at birthday parties, but these toys quickly found their way into a bag at the back of the closet and eventually out the door. I wanted my daughters to grow up dreaming of one day becoming a wife to a godly husband, and be a mom who would be intentional about raising up a godly heritage. I still pray for that daily.

When I went shopping for my kids the first Christmas after we adopted Karis, I went to the toy store to find the biggest, softest, cuddliest black and white newborn dolls in the store, and brought them home to put under the tree for my "brown sugar" and my "white sugar." I wanted them to enjoy being little girls as long as they could, and not to grow up prematurely.

I am grateful that Trinity, now a seventeen year old, is still choosing to be a godly woman with discriminating tastes. She has turned down R-rated movies in two situations this week–once at the theatre with friends where she ended up in a different movie sitting by herself, and just last night at a sleepover where she chose to stay in her friend's bedroom and spend time with the Lord until her friends finished watching their video.

The old saying that "birds of a feather flock together" holds true. It is important for us to help our children develop strong, godly friendships. This requires concerted prayer more than anything else. We have the greatest influence in helping our children select their friends when they are quite young. You must do this deliberately, because most neighborhoods pull against this. Ours certainly have. There have been times when we've had to step in and separate unhealthy friendships with every one of our five children. But later on down the road, we were always grateful that we did.

One of the best ways to help your children find positive peers is to be involved in a church or Christian school with a strong youth program and good ministries available to the kids. Teens need a spiritual environment where they feel comfortable to thrive and grow during these years. You may need to change churches to accomplish this, but you will one day see the reward of any sacrifice or inconvenience.

It is also important to have an "open home" policy where your children's friends are always welcome. I can't begin to tell you how many carpet spots we've scrubbed up or how many rings we still have on our furniture. And yet it's been worth it to see how God has ministered to literally hundreds of teens over the past decade in our home.

Moms, don't wring your hands over your kids. Instead, fold your hands in prayer and do something active in your children's lives. There is a little known Scripture in Isaiah 62: 10 that encourages us to go through the gates and do something positive.

Go through,
Go through the gates!
Prepare the way for the people;
Build up,
Build up the highway!

Take out the stones,
Lift up a banner for the peoples!

I have had the joy of leading some of my kids' friends to the Lord over the years. When we moved to Orlando, we knew the home He gave us belonged to Him, which meant He could use it in whatever ways He desired. When our three sons were in high school, we had as many as eighty teens in our home every week. In middle school, the girls hosted a weekly Bible study in our house, since many of our neighborhood girls couldn't go all the way to church with us. (At the time, it was eighteen miles away.) For the past few years, we have had the area Student Venture (Campus Crusade for Christ's student ministry) meetings on Monday nights, and the kids pack in like sardines. All of our children have served as emcees, worship leaders, guitar players, skit participants, rap artists, speakers—whatever was needed at the time.

Jason's best friend in high school was James, a boy I'd had the joy of leading to Christ in our van one day on the way home from church when he was a middle-school student. He is now studying to be a pastor and is married to the daughter of a pastor. What a joy and delight to watch God work in these kids' lives. As they watch you, they learn accordingly. Now our children lead their own friends to Christ. What a fulfilling way to work yourself out of a job.

The last half hour of their day was, and is, our children's time with God. Once they entered high school they were given more freedom, but even then I would gently remind them from time to time when I saw them slipping. How it warmed my heart to see our sons continue in the Word of God, prayer, and discipleship when they went away to college.

"How can a young man cleanse his way?
By taking heed according to Your word.
With my whole heart I have sought You;
Oh, let me not wander from Your commandments!
Your word I have hidden in my heart,
That I might not sin against You" (Psalm 119:9-11).

What will keep us, as well as our children, from sin? *Nothing* but the Word of God. The wonderful result of trust and obedience is peace.

"Open the gates,
That the righteous nation which keeps the truth may enter in.
You will keep him in perfect peace,
Whose mind is stayed on You,
Because he trusts in You" (Isaiah 26:2-3).

Tabernacle Truth

"Stand in the gate of the Lord's house, and proclaim there this word, and say, 'Hear the word of the Lord!'" "Amend your ways and your doings, and I will cause you to dwell in this place" (Jeremiah 7:2a, 3b).

We are all to be gatekeepers over our eyes and ears, the gateway to our souls. We parents are to be gatekeepers for our children until they are able to gradually take over that responsibility for themselves. What we focus on is what we will become. The same is true for them. We must carefully pull those weeds of sin when we first see them pop through the soil, because little weeds grow into big weeds that eventually suck the life out of us—and our children.

Open to me the gates of righteousness;
I will go through them,
And I will praise the Lord.
This is the gate of the Lord,
Through which the righteous shall enter (Psalm 118:19-20).

I want to close with a special poem that has been on my refrigerator for many years. It is still there to this day, though it has grown yellow with age. There is a precious little note in the margin written by my sweet, sensitive second-born son, Jason, during his early teen years. It reads, simply, "Jason loves his Mom." If you have children at home, perhaps you will feel led to make a copy for your fridge door.

<u>A Child is for Molding</u>

I took a piece of plastic clay,
And idly fashioned it one day,
And as my fingers pressed it still,
It bent and yielded to my will.

I came again when days were past,
The bit of clay was hard at last,
The form I gave it still it bore,
But I could change that form no more.

I took a piece of living clay,
And gently formed it day by day,
And molded it with power and art
A young child's soft and yielded heart.

I came again when years were gone:
He was a man I looked upon.
The early imprint still he bore,
But I could change him then no more.
Anonymous

Points to Ponder and Pray

May we courageously follow the example of Susannah Wesley and be diligent with the little things. We must remember that Jesus said, "Enter by the narrow gate; for wide is the gate and broad is the way that leads to destruction, and there are many who go in by it. Because narrow is the gate and difficult is the way which leads to life, and there are few who find it" (Matthew 7:13-14).

What is the Lord asking you to begin doing for yourself or your children? What is He asking you to stop doing? Where have you been neglectful? What things do you need to commit to prayer?

Please don't turn the page until you have taken time to sort this out before your Father in heaven. Take out a notebook and prayerfully make a list of the things He is putting on your heart. Make this your prayer list during the coming months. As you pray and obey, you will be amazed at the miracles God will accomplish in your home and family.

Chapter 11

Laurie Steen Killingsworth?

I met Tipton David Killingsworth ("Tip," to his friends and "Tippy" to his family) the first week I set foot on the Arizona State University campus. We were introduced by one of his fraternity brothers after the first football game of the 1967 season. I was a "very mature" twenty-year old and he, in my opinion, was an immature nineteen-year old. Needless to say, our relationship didn't start off with a bang. However, I continued to cross paths with him at Campus Crusade for Christ meetings and fraternity functions, and I dated some of his fraternity brothers who were Christians.

In January of 1969 God began to turn my heart toward Tip in a new way, and I wrestled with Him over the matter for months. By the end of May I finally came to a place of peace, as I understood that God was directing me toward making a life commitment. I was just beginning to learn what it meant to be submissive to the will of God *and* to a man. There was no stronger-willed young woman on the face of the earth than *this* one.

We began our life journey together in a beautiful candlelit church in Scottsdale, Arizona, on June 6, 1970. When I went to the altar to meet the handsome young man whom God had clearly shown me I was to marry, he was all of twenty-two, and I was five days short of twenty-three. We both felt quite mature. After all, I'd been on my own for a year traveling with *The New Folk,* and Tip had graduated from college just four days before our wedding. We knew we loved each other and were confidant that we could handle any curve ball life might throw us.

It didn't take long for reality to set in. Just three days after the wedding, on our way to San Bernardino, California, our little blue four-cylinder Chevy Nova's engine seized at the Arizona/California border, and stopped dead in its tracks. As I sat alone in a cheap little motel room for three days and three nights in the hot, dusty town of Blythe, I felt like Jonah in the belly of the big fish. I also spent my twenty-third birthday there, which turned out to be one of the biggest non-events of my life. All of our wedding money was eaten up on fixing that car along with most of my high hopes for our new life together. During the first few weeks of our marriage, I questioned many times this life-changing commitment I'd made.

Our years together have seen many ups and downs, including some really rough patches from time to time. We have now experienced three decades of growth as a couple.

Growth is not the product of effort, but of life. Even though Tip and I are very different in temperament, we both have strong, determined personalities. He has a sanguine temperament, and I am a choleric. You could say that he is an otter and I am a lion. He loves to play, and I love to get things done. You can see how the rub can easily set in.

To be honest, there have been many times over the years that I have fleetingly thought of bailing out. (Frankly, I've never met a married person who hasn't.) But God has shown me time after time that He is more interested in working through the situations than in me giving up and starting over. Tip is a wonderful man of God who has taught me more about unconditional love than any person on the planet. In spite of this, I often end up praying, "God, just help me to love him!" Since you are a sinner just like I am, I bet you can identify with that.

God longs for us to have strong, fulfilling marriages. He wants us to raise a godly heritage that will go on after us to fulfill His purposes in the world. How grateful I am that He is always strong when I am weak, and that He is always faithful, even when I'm not. He is the God of forgiveness and restoration, continually making all things new.

The Lord is very clear in His Word what His standard and purpose are for marriage. As you read this passage of Scripture, do a quick analysis of your own marriage.

"He (God) does not regard the offering anymore,
Nor receive it with goodwill from your hands.
Yet you say, "For what reason?"
Because the Lord has been witness
Between you and the wife of your youth,
With whom you have dealt treacherously;
Yet she is your companion
And your wife by covenant.
But did He not make them one,
Having a remnant of the Spirit?
And why one?
He seeks godly offspring.
Therefore take heed to your spirit,
And let none deal treacherously with the wife of his youth.

"For the Lord God of Israel says
That He hates divorce,
For it covers one's garment with violence,"
Says the Lord of hosts.
"Therefore take heed to your spirit,
That you do not deal treacherously" (Malachi 2:13b-16, emphasis mine).

This is our covenant together as man and wife with God, and our corporate purpose in life. Note that He made us one with a remnant of the Spirit because *He seeks godly offspring.* As we consider our nation's problems with our youth, we need look no further than the breakdown of the family.

As you read through the following warning signs of divorce, ask God to show you where your marriage needs attention:

Dullness
Independence
Vexation of immaturity
Omission of God
Romance fizzles
Communication breakdown
Entrapped by materialism

The tidal wave of divorce continues to crash over the family structure in the western world, and even many Christians are being engulfed and swept away. The most recent report from the Barna Research Group found that the percentage of born again adults who have been married and divorced is very similar to that of non-born again adults. I find it sad that those who profess the name of Christ behave no differently from the world. Even as I write, Tip and I are counseling a number of people who are struggling with Christian counselors who are encouraging spouses to seek divorce, ignoring the Word of God.

The writings of King Solomon, the wisest man who ever lived, continue to warn each passing generation.

> Do not be rash with your mouth,
> And let not your heart utter anything hastily before God.
> For God is in heaven, and you on earth;
> Therefore let your words be few.
> For a dream comes through much activity,
> And a fool's voice is known by his many words.
>
> When you make a vow to God, do not delay to pay it;
> For He has no pleasure in fools.
> Pay what you have vowed–
> Better not to vow than to vow and not pay.
>
> Do not let your mouth cause your flesh to sin, nor say before the messenger of God that it was an error. ... But fear God (Ecclesiastes 5:2-6a, 7b).

I have searched the Bible, but I can't find any legitimate reason for divorce other than adultery.

> The Pharisees also came to Him, testing Him, and saying to Him, "Is it lawful for a man to divorce his wife for just any reason?" And He answered and said to them, "Have you not read that He who made them at the beginning 'made them male and female,' and said, 'For this reason a man shall leave his father and mother and be joined to his wife, and the two

> shall become one flesh'? So then, they are no longer two but one flesh. Therefore what God has joined together, let not man separate."
> He said to them, "Moses, because of the hardness of your hearts, permitted you to divorce your wives, but from the beginning it was not so. And I say to you, whoever divorces his wife, except for sexual immorality, and marries another, commits adultery; and whoever marries her who is divorced commits adultery" (Matthew 19:3-6, 8-9).

We live in a culture with such an "instant pudding" mentality that commitment seems to have become a dirty word. Often the problems in our marriages are our own fault because we do not love our spouses the way that Christ commands us to.

Try this little test. Put your name in place of the word *love* in First Corinthians 13: 4-8a, and determine *your* marital or relational temperature.

> Love suffers long and is kind; love does not envy; love does not parade itself, is not puffed up; does not behave rudely, does not seek its own, is not provoked, thinks no evil; does not rejoice in iniquity, but rejoices in the truth; bears all things, believes all things, hopes all things, endures all things. Love never fails.

Love is not about chemistry or feelings. Often, the reason the *feeling* of being in love disappears is because we're not *doing* what the Bible tells us to. I would encourage you to spend some time reading the following chapters in the Bible: First Peter 3, Ephesians 5, First Timothy 2-3, and Titus 2. These have very specific instructions for wives and how they are to relate to their husbands. If we do our part, God will do His part. If we show our spouses admiration, honor, and respect, it won't be long before we begin to see change. For one thing, we will find that *feelings* of love for our mate will begin to grow and develop.

As we become obedient to God in these areas, our mates will begin to feel more loving toward us. They will begin to treat us differently, and desire to spend more time with us. It's cyclical. I'm convinced, through much personal trial and error, that if we go God's way, our marriages can be strong and satisfying. Believe me, I have tried every wrong way to relate to my mate and I continue to learn daily how to make life's most difficult, yet most rewarding relationship work.

How can we walk in wisdom and maturity with our spouses and others? What is maturity anyway? It's all about relying on God, rather than on self. The more times we trust Him, the more we grow toward maturity. The value of marriage is not just that adults produce children, but that children produce adults.

When our children are small, their focus and trust is wholly on us. It is our job as parents to see that they learn how to transfer that trust from us to their heavenly Father. By the same token, if we are focusing on our own wants, needs, and desires most of the time, we'll tend to trust ourselves. If we focus more on another person, we will transfer our trust to them and expect them to meet our needs. Our single focus and passion must be on the only One who is always there, always able, and totally trustworthy.

Many of us live our Christian lives consciously looking for ways to serve and be more devoted to God. Our goal is not to intentionally act like a Christian, but to simply live in a love relationship with our Bridegroom. This same truth should be followed in our marriages.

To achieve this, we must spend time in His Word and with His people. Our focus must be on the Lord. His thoughts become our thoughts as we spend time hearing, reading, and studying His Word. That is what causes our trust to transfer to Him, where it needs to be. Jesus promised us an exchanged life—ours for His—but it's our choice whether or not to make the trade. When we stop growing, we stop living and settle for merely existing. This affects our spiritual lives first, but then bleeds over into our marriages and families.

The first and most obvious place to practice this principle is within our own homes, our "greenhouse" for growth.

Now is your God-given opportunity to choose where you will place your focus. What is going on in your relationships at home and beyond? As they say, the biggest room in the world is the room for improvement. We will never *arrive* until we go home to be with the Lord.

Not that I have already attained, or am already perfected; but

I press on, that I may lay hold of that for which Christ Jesus has also laid hold of me. Brethren, I do not count myself to have apprehended; but one thing I do, *forgetting those things which are behind and reaching forward to those things which are ahead, I press toward the goal for the prize of the upward call of God in Christ Jesus* (Philippians 3:12-15, emphasis mine).

Tabernacle Truth

"And the Lord God said, "It is not good that man should be alone; I will make him a helper comparable to him" (Genesis 2:18). Marriage is not just a good idea that our society came up with at some point; it is the divine design that originated in the heart of God. It was God Who created Adam, and it was God who brought the woman to Adam, joined the two together, and said, "Therefore a man shall leave his father and mother and be joined to his wife, and they shall become one flesh" (2:24).

As God by creation made two of one, so again by marriage he made one of two. One plus one equals one may not be an accurate mathematical concept, but it is an accurate description of God's intention for the marriage relationship. A man's children are pieces of himself, but his wife is himself.

But it must go a step further. A successful marriage is always a triangle: a man, a woman, and God. Three is the number of the trinity and unity throughout the Bible. Because it was all God's idea in the first place, that is the primary reason that it just isn't possible to pull it off without His help. God did not create woman to be a competitor, but a companion. A great marriage is not a destination; it is a daily work in progress.

Don't be discouraged if you haven't arrived. Neither have I. It is a commitment that we renew daily, just as we do in our relationship with our heavenly Bridegroom. Marriage is an audio-visual of what our relationship with Jesus Christ should be. That's why we must realize that it *is* important and it *was* created to last. As we walk in this commitment we need to learn to love and live to give – just as Jesus does.

I'm sure you've heard the saying that the grass may appear greener on the other side of the fence, but you still have to mow it. Well, you can also bet the water bill is higher. Some marriages may have been made in heaven, but they *all* have to be maintained on earth. A successful marriage is an edifice that must be rebuilt every day.

Remember that success in marriage is much more than finding the right person; it is a matter of being the right person. We often hear that marriage is a 50/50 compromise, but that is not true. If we don't give it all we've got, there will usually be a deficiency along the way. With 50/50 there's no space for error, but with each giving their all, we have room to be human and still hit 100%.

A marriage is like a long trip in a tiny rowboat: If one passenger starts to rock the boat, the other has to steady it; otherwise they will go to the bottom together. Don't look around for a life partner, look up. Any other choice than God's can only spell trouble.

I am so grateful that God and Tip have never given up on me. Tip was my best friend in 1970 when I walked down the aisle to meet him at the altar and he is my best friend now.

There is a treasure waiting to be discovered within each one of us, as well as in our marriages, as we are filled and controlled by the Holy Spirit. The mining of that wealth takes a lifetime, but it is so worth it.

Chains do not hold a marriage together. It is threads, hundreds of tiny threads that are woven together through the years. One day all of those seemingly tangled threads will disappear as God turns that tapestry over to reveal a beautiful creation of art.

Points to Ponder and Pray

The best use of life is love, the best expression of love is time, and the best time to love is now. Please take a few minutes to think about what changes God is prompting you to make in your life and, if you are married, in your relationship with your husband.

Try surrendering your will to God, and allow His Spirit to daily lead you in working toward healing in your marriage. When we replace our complaining with prayer, we will see amazing things happen. Keep in mind that a few right choices will not undo many years of wrong ones. Do not jump ship before you reach your new world.

When we pray, we tap into the richest resource in the universe available to us 24/7/365. Sometimes when we pray for people, they often get worse before they get better. The same is true with us. It's during this time that we are tempted to quit trying. Be patient and let God do His work. God will reward you for it; I guarantee it.

Where are you now? Where do you desire to be at this time next year? No one can do this for you. The choice is yours.

Chapter 12

Looking for Love in all the Wrong Places

"You and Jason are wonderful gifts from the Lord, Trey," I said to my three-year old son. "We prayed for you to come!"

He looked up at me thoughtfully and said, "I was in Jesus, and Jason was in Jesus, and you and Daddy were alone. Then Jason and I came down."

My interest piqued, I asked, "How did you come, Trey?" He looked at me confidently and replied, "We came down a ladder!"

Our children's baby books are full of these growing perceptions of love, marriage, babies, and how it all works. They make for great reading and lots of laughs.

One evening at the dinner table, when Trey was six, he piped up out of the blue with "How does the sperm get from the daddy to the egg in the mommy? Is it in the swimming pool where it floats in the water?"

With my fork poised in midair, I nearly choked. Then I assured him that "God has a very special way, Sweetheart" and changed the subject.

Still pondering this subject two weeks later, he said, "I know! The mommy and daddy stand heart to heart! Is that right?"

Tip and I concluded that he was wise beyond his years. God, the One who created it all in the first place, desires that a husband and a wife bond "heart to heart" through sex.

To get a fuller picture of what that means, read the Song of Solomon in the Old Testament. It contains the most passionate, symbolic language you'll ever read. And it's the best-selling book on romance ever written.

Just to whet your appetite, these eight brief chapters begin with:

> Let him kiss me with the kisses of his mouth–
> For your love is better than wine.
> Because of the fragrance of your good ointments,
> Your name is ointment poured forth (1:2-3a).

Neglecting sex in our marriages can give Satan a foot in the door. That's why Paul wrote:

> It is good for a man not to touch a woman. Nevertheless, because of sexual immorality, let each man have his own wife, and let each woman have her own husband. Let the husband render to his wife the affection due her, and likewise also the wife to her husband. The wife does not have authority over her own body, but the husband does. And likewise the husband does not have authority over his own body, but the wife does. Do not deprive one another (1 Corinthians 7:1b-5a).

I recommend reading all of chapters six and seven of First Corinthians for a clearer picture of God's heart for us in this area.

In many marriages, Christian and otherwise, wives are often attracted to other men, and husbands are attracted to other women. Christian women are hesitant to admit this, yet whenever I conduct a conference, women share with me their struggle in this area.

There was a time in my own marriage when I felt an attraction for a man who had been a close friend for many years. My first desire was to meet his spiritual needs, but that eventually presented a serious danger. The more spiritually close you are to a person; the deeper the level of intimacy. Emotional intimacy with anyone other than your spouse leads to emotional infidelity, and emotional infidelity can lead to physical infidelity. Thankfully, I was able to lead my friend to Christ. But this is often the path Satan uses to destroy otherwise healthy marriages.

> Likewise you younger people, submit yourselves to your elders. Yes, all of you be submissive to one another, and be clothed with humility, for "God resists the proud, but gives grace to the humble." Therefore humble yourselves under the mighty hand of God, that He may exalt you in due time, casting all your care upon Him, for He cares for you. Be sober, be vigilant; because your adversary the devil walks about like a roaring lion, seeking whom he may devour. *Resist him*, steadfast in the faith, knowing that the same sufferings are experienced by your brotherhood in the world. But may the God of all grace, who called us to His eternal glory by Christ Jesus, after you have suffered a while, perfect, establish, strengthen, and settle you (1 Peter 5:5-10, emphasis mine).

When we fall into the traps Satan sets for us, we not only hurt ourselves but also the lives and futures of those who follow us. If you find yourself in a tempting situation with the opposite sex, take radical measures to avoid making a mistake that will negatively impact you and your family for the rest of your life and beyond. Move to a different neighborhood. Change your job, your doctor, your pool man, even your church, if necessary. Do whatever it takes to put distance between yourself and that person, not only geographically, but also emotionally.

Once we allow Satan to conquer territory in our lives, it requires time and aggressive warfare to gain it back. This pulling down of strongholds is not accomplished instantaneously. It is a process. We don't get into these situations in a day, nor do we get out of them in a day. Such an attraction can keep you distracted for a long time.

Satan doesn't care *how* he derails us as long as he gets us off track. He will use our best intentions and our dearest friendships to attack our marriages and wreak havoc in our lives.

If you think this warning is irrelevant and could never apply to you, think again. The Kinsey Report indicates that approximately 50 percent of married people have been unfaithful at some point during their marriage. Sex is a big deal in our culture today because it's the closest substitute for a spiritual experience that some people will ever taste. Never forget that only Jesus can fill an empty heart.

It is said that our eyes are the windows to our soul. Where is our focus? What are we feeding on? Television, movies, videos, DVDs, magazines, and secular romance novels influence our minds and hearts more than we may realize. Satan loves this because, once he gets our focus off of Jesus, he can effectively neutralize us. There is only one Bridegroom who can satisfy our deepest longings. We are "betrothed" to Him, and we eagerly await the wedding feast of the Lamb. Are you ready for that day?

A person is not what he thinks he is. Rather, *what a person thinks, he is*. Those who don't make themselves accountable to anyone are more likely to find themselves in dangerous, tempting circumstances. Find someone who is willing to be your mentor or prayer partner. Engage in group activities with friends, rather than alone.

Be jealous of your time. Life is too short to do everything *we* want to do, but it is long enough for us to do everything *God* wants us to do.

King Solomon, reputedly the wisest man who ever lived, warns us:

> Give attention to my words;
> Incline your *ear* to my sayings.
> Do not let them depart from your *eyes*;
> Keep them in the midst of your *heart*;
> For they are life to those who find them,
> And health to all their *flesh*.
> *Keep your heart with all diligence,*
> *For out of it spring the issues of life*" (Proverbs 4:20-23, emphasis mine).

Be careful what you set your heart on, for that desire will surely become yours. The Bible is full of lessons on the heart.

> Blessed is the man who trusts in the Lord,
> And whose hope is the Lord.
> For he shall be like a tree planted by the waters,
> Which spreads out its roots by the river,
> And will not fear when heat comes;
> But its leaf will be green,
> And will not be anxious in the year of drought,
> Nor will cease from yielding fruit.

> The *heart* is deceitful above all things,
> And desperately wicked;
> Who can know it?
> I, the Lord, search the heart,
> I test the mind (Jeremiah 17:7-10a, emphasis mine).

When we find a battle going on in our minds or hearts, we must understand how to fight it. The Scriptures give us a plan of attack.

> For though we walk in the flesh, we do not war according to the flesh. For the weapons of our warfare are not carnal but mighty in God for pulling down strongholds, casting down arguments and every high thing that exalts itself against the knowledge of God, bringing every thought into captivity to the obedience of Christ (2 Corinthians 10:3-5)

I keep a little paper inside my portfolio that reads:

Sow a thought, and you reap an act,
Sow an act, and you reap a habit,
Sow a habit, and you reap a character,
Sow a character, and you reap a destiny.
Anonymous

When we realize just how many people we impact, we begin to get the picture of how crucial it is that we sit up and take notice. How many parents have pointed fingers at their children and said, "Do as I say, not as I do"? This is not a joke, nor will it work. With children things are more often "caught" than "taught."

You can see why it is so important that we live holy lives. What is purity, anyway? It's a word we don't even really use much anymore. Christians have an obligation to show the world that purity of body, soul, and spirit is not only possible, but essential. Jesus was the embodiment of purity. He was pure in spirit (morality), in behavior (integrity), in relationships (virtue), and in practice (authenticity). That is certainly what I desire for my life. How about you?

But it's easier said than done, isn't it? I am far from perfect on all of these counts, and I suspect you are too. Our pastor for ten years, Jim Henry, said that "your reputation is your photo; your character is your face." When people look at you, do they see your photo or your face?

I once taught a quarterly sexual intimacy class for women who were going through our church's marriage preparation course. When I started, I was surprised that a sizable chunk of each class were there for second and third marriages, and that many are already living with the men they were not yet married to. These weren't couples off the street, but members of a strong, evangelical church body. We live in a society where people have ceased valuing marriage vows, submission, or fidelity.

After our children hit their thirteenth birthdays, we start taking them out for dinner once a year and present them with small, decorative boxes containing our dreams and goals for their lives for that year (spiritually, mentally, physically, and academically). As we enjoyed this special meal together, Tip and I encourage them to provide input. It's a five-year countdown that ends at their eighteenth birthday with a launching-out into the world.

Parents need to talk to their kids about everything in their lives, including the importance of sexual purity. I began talking about this with my children at a very young age. When they turned sixteen, we presented Trey, Jason, Josh, and Trinity with purity rings. At that time, each of them made a covenant of purity before God and us. Karis renewed her covenant of purity on her seventeenth birthday. It's never too late to get a fresh start with God, no matter where you are or have been in your life.

Not one of us is perfect. If our children should fall in this area, we need to show them love and forgiveness, just as Jesus did with the woman caught in adultery. "He who is without sin among you, let him throw a stone at her first" (John 8:7b). When your children fall, be the first to step forward and put your arms around them. Let them know that God loves them and forgives them, yet still longs for them to begin to walk in obedience and purity.

How can we protect our children? I have found that many Christian parents are naive about the most basic issues of godly parenting. A generation ago we had a lot of help from the community and the church to help our children learn right from wrong. This is no longer the case. But we can still gain a wealth of knowledge if we take the time to look in the right places. One of my favorites is my local Christian bookstore. There are a number of good books available out there for teens on purity, dating, relationships, and any other issue that they may be facing. Over the past decade I have purchased many such books for my teenagers.

The Lord holds our relationship with Him jealously. He wants our passion to be "single" for Him. This is true all the way through the Bible, and is even emphasized in the first of the Ten Commandments: "You shall have no other gods before Me" (Exodus 20:3, 23; 34:14). All of the other commandments hinge on the first and greatest one. If we encourage our teens to "date around," we are breaking down the very principle that will give them strength in both their physical and spiritual lives as they mature. The marriage relationship is an audio-visual representation to the world of what our relationship with God should be. There is one man for every woman, and it is God's responsibility to bring those persons together when the time is right, just as He did with Eve and Adam. Manipulating the circumstances or "working the odds" is not only unnecessary, but shows a lack of faith.

Giving good books to our kids is helpful as we challenge them to wait for God's choice in a life mate. Dating is a concept developed by man, not by God. It encourages their hearts to wander. Let's teach our children to develop friendships with the opposite sex in groups, not in isolated settings, for their own protection.

Have them sit out of sex-education classes at school. When they come home with those permission slips, don't sign them. (In the Appendix you will find an official opt-out form that you may want to use.) What they become comfortable talking about with others is often what they want to experiment with. It's preferable to spend that hour in study hall or doing whatever is offered as an alternative. This type of instruction should begin and end at home.

Would you let your son or daughter go off with a complete stranger? "Of course not!" you say. Well, think about how teens tend to date. They get a call and the next thing you know someone is honking the horn and waiting in his or her car. Now, consider that stranger example again. When you send your child off on a date with someone you don't know, it's the same thing. So make sure you know whom your child is spending time with. Try to meet their parents. Invite the child to spend time with your family at home before the date. Be aware of what's going on in your child's dating life.

I have become radical on the subject of courtship. Jason (our second son) and his best friend, James (my spiritual son), wrote papers during the summer before their senior year in high school on "Emotional Abstinence: Adopting God's Plan as our Own." They would be the first to tell you that they didn't always follow their own advice, and yet they strongly believe that this is God's plan as taught in the Word of God. Josh (our third son) wrote a paper during his first year of college on "Courtship: The Answer to a Successful Marriage." (You will find all three of these papers in the Appendix.)

Staying physically abstinent is extremely difficult for even the strongest of kids unless they go a step further by not getting involved emotionally in the first place.

Shortly before his fourth birthday, Jason looked at a passerby one day and said, "I'm going to give that lady a kiss. I love all the ladies in the world!" That fall, when he started school (they start at four in Ireland), he came home and said, "I love my teacher. I forgot to kiss her, but tomorrow I'll kiss her!" On yet another occasion, while driving around with his dad, he looked out the car window and wistfully said, "Dad, I have a problem at school." Tip asked him what it was, thinking it must be very serious. Jason said with even greater seriousness, "There isn't one girl in my class who will marry me!" Tip struggled to keep from laughing out loud, but yes, Jason seemed to have only one thing on his mind. After a dozen more years of growth, he penned these words:

Somewhere

Somewhere in the night,
She shuts her eyes to rest.
Moonlight plays across her angelic face
And dreams are movies in her mind.

This young woman is growing fast,
Watching her childhood years slip past.

Chosen by God to share my life
As a mother and a wife.

Our love will grow with each passing day,
Come what will and come what may.
I pray that she remains pure
In spirit and in flesh.

Living for Him whom we both adore,
This is my prayer, Lord.
Protect her and keep her in the palm of Your hand.
Someday we'll work together to heal our land.

Tabernacle Truth

Our goal in our journey through the Tabernacle is to find our way into the Holy of Holies. Only there will we find intimacy that will meet our deepest needs. He is the only One who knows those needs because He created us. Settling for anything less is settling for a counterfeit that will not satisfy. Our marriages here on earth are simply a living picture of a spiritual truth. That's why it's so important that we get it right!

Points to Ponder and Pray

What can you do today to get your marriage or relationship on a more solid footing? What can you do with your children to help to prepare them for a pure transition into marriage? How can you rescue them if they have already fallen?

Consider writing down what God is saying to you, and use it as your ongoing prayer list in the coming months. Persevere until you see change.

Chapter 13

A Place Called Simplicity

When Tip and I felt God calling us to Ireland, we'd been married for four years. At the encouragement of some friends who were already missionaries in Europe, we decided to free ourselves from the shackles of material possessions as much as possible. We were living in Tulsa, Oklahoma, at the time, doing advance work for the Athletes in Action weightlifting team, and living in a 14' x 70' mobile home in the country. We started by selling the mobile home and unloading many of our belongings through garage sales. When we left for Ireland, we had our suitcases, two small barrels of household goods, and our books and tapes. What a wonderful feeling! It was so freeing to have all our worldly goods in such a small space. Off we went, with a promised salary of $500 per month ... *if* we could raise it, that is.

We did raise our support, and off we went to Galway, on the west side of Ireland. Six years later, God called us to move to Dublin, which is on the east side. We had two young sons, a house full of second-hand furniture, and a stockpile of acquired toys and other toddler paraphernalia. It doesn't take long to accumulate *stuff*, does it? It took us two trips with a large truck to accomplish the move.

I can tell you from experience, though, that it's a joy to live simply. We need to be willing to look at material things the way God does.

Do you need a house? Pray for a house. God provided a lovely home for us in Orlando when we had no money for a down payment or equity from a previous home. Miracle after miracle brought it to pass.

Do you need a car? Pray for a car. God has given us (and our teenagers) five cars since we returned from Ireland in 1986. Friends, at a price considerably below market value, sold two others to us.

Do you need clothes? Again, pray for what you need. I had a black pantsuit on my prayer list a few years ago. One day, a wealthy friend unexpectedly pulled one out of her closet ... in my size, with the tags still on it. When she asked me if I wanted it, I nearly fainted ... especially when I looked at the tags! It was made in Paris, was 100 percent wool, and she had paid almost $2,000 for it.

These are just a few examples on a lifetime list of answered prayers. Let God be the God of your life. He is eagerly waiting for His children to ask. He doesn't always say yes, but He does always listen, answering according to His will.

He wants us to be generous people with giving hearts. Our family has been the recipient of support, in both prayer and finances, by very special people for over thirty years. We, in turn, like to give generously because we've been blessed extravagantly.

How much should you be giving? The amount is a matter between you and God. He just wants us to give joyfully, as unto the Lord. He will greatly bless you as you give Him what is rightfully His in tithes, and beyond that, in offerings.

Malachi 3 is like the "Pepsi Challenge" of living a life of generosity.

> "Will a man rob God?
> Yet you have robbed Me!
> But you say,
> 'In what way have we robbed You?'
> 'In tithes and offerings.
> You are cursed with a curse,
> For you have robbed Me,
> Even this whole nation.
> Bring all the tithes into the storehouse,
> That there may be food in My house,
> And try Me now in this,"
> Says the Lord of hosts,
> If I will not open for you the windows of heaven
> And pour out for you such blessing
> That there will not be room enough to receive it.

> And I will rebuke the devourer for your sakes (3:8-11a).

We have "lived on love" now for over three decades, and it's not usually the wealthy who are the most generous. The "deceitfulness of riches" can drag us down and choke the fruitfulness out of our lives, regardless of our income level.

You may say, "But I'm not wealthy. I'm just average middle-class." When any of us compares ourselves with the vast majority of the world, we *are* wealthy. If we have more than one change of clothing, and we have enough food in our home for more than one day, we are wealthy. "Now he who received seed among the thorns is he who hears the word, and the cares of this world and the *deceitfulness of riches* choke the word, and he becomes unfruitful" (Matthew 13:22, emphasis mine).

Jesus admonishes us in the Sermon on the Mount,

> "Therefore do not worry, saying, 'What shall we eat?' or 'What shall we drink?' or 'What shall we wear?' For after all these things the Gentiles seek. For your heavenly Father knows that you need all these things. *But seek first the kingdom of God and His righteousness, and all these things shall be added to you.* Therefore do not worry about tomorrow" (Matthew 6:31-34a, emphasis mine).

Are we living simply? We assume, usually without really considering it deeply, that what the world tells us will satisfy us, and so that is what we should seek. Often those things do nothing but weigh us down. It's like having an anchor tied to our ankles as we attempt to swim. Material things can be a dead weight to real joy, rather than a buoy to keep us afloat. The accumulation of more "things" to clean, dust, repair, service, store, and keep up with often just adds stress to our lives. What many Christians are missing is the beauty of a simple lifestyle.

The Bible talks more about generosity and giving than all other virtues combined. Hope is mentioned 185 times, faith 246 times, love 733 times, and giving 2,285 times! The majority of Jesus' parables have to do with money and the use of it. He wants us to "get it" and not fall into the enticing trap of a materialistic lifestyle. We all need to be continually reminded to be good stewards of what God gives us, to work on living debt free, and to become more generous in our giving.

The Apostle Paul challenged us to excel in giving, using the churches of Macedonia as an example:

> Beyond their ability, they were freely willing, imploring us with much urgency that we would *receive the gift* and the fellowship of the ministering to the saints. And not only as we had hoped, but *they first gave themselves to the Lord, and then to us* by the will of God. But as you abound in everything—in faith, in speech, in knowledge, in all diligence, and in your love for us—see that you abound in this grace also. For if there is first a willing mind, it is accepted according to what one has, and not according to what he does not have. For I do not mean that others should be eased and you burdened; but by an equality, that now at this time your abundance may supply their lack, that their abundance also may supply your lack—that there may be equality (2 Corinthians 8:3b-5, 7, 12-14, emphasis mine).

In the next chapter, Paul goes on to say,

> He who sows sparingly will also reap sparingly, and he who sows bountifully will also reap bountifully. So let each one give as he purposes in his heart, not grudgingly or of necessity; for *God loves a cheerful giver*. And God is able to make *all* grace abound toward you, that you, always having *all* sufficiency in *all* things, may have an abundance for *every* good work (2 Corinthians 9:6-8, emphasis mine).

The law of reciprocity states that whatever you want more of, give in that area. If you want more kindness, give more kindness. If you want more love, give more love. If I do this, God will do that.

As we simplify the way we live, we also need to simplify the way we speak to others and to God. To amplify what I have written in a previous chapter, the Bible says there is strife in many words. We are to let our yes be yes and our no be no (Matthew 5:37). As we practice this with others, it will help us be more straightforward with our heavenly Father as well. He isn't interested in hearing our liturgical memorized prayers or our pious platitudes. He desires to hear our hearts. Pour out your heart before Him with no pretense, and your intimacy with Him will grow without measure.

As our words become less complicated, so will our actions. Very simply, God wants us to love others from a pure heart and serve them with humility. Many Christians are not living simply, are not content, and do not trust God to provide. His goal is that we simplify the way we live so that we will experience rest. "He said to them, 'Come aside by yourselves to a deserted place and rest a while'" (Mark 6:31). We need to accept our limitations and put space in our schedules by removing unnecessary activity from our lives. As we do less, we trust God more. Even Jesus, who was perfect in every way, built margins and space into His life.

Let's take the hurry out of our hurried lifestyle. Busyness causes us to feel more stress, lose our joy, be less productive, and crowd out the voice of God. This is why God commands us to take one day of rest for every six days that we work. We need to simplify our pace, stop the constant push for more, and learn to say no. God's timing is perfect. He is never early, never late, always on time.

To simplify our lives, we must be willing to let go of whatever we're hanging on to. We can't reach forward with our arms open wide in expectancy until we have first released what we're clutching. We must let go of the old traditions, attitudes, ways of thinking, and even some of our relationships. Let's move on to what God wants us to be as we release the old and take hold of the new. "Therefore, if anyone is in Christ, he is a new creation; old things have passed away; behold, all things have become new" (2 Corinthians 5:17). Forget past sins and live today without guilt about yesterday. We don't kill the flesh by beating it up; we kill it by not feeding it.

The best way to release is to learn to *give*—of our time, our talent, and our treasure. As we do, the benefits are limitless. We will be more like God and will be drawn closer to Him as our faith is strengthened. The grip of materialism will be broken in our lives when we stop believing that our self-worth is connected to our net worth. We will be blessed immeasurably as we make investments for eternity. We will be happier as givers than as takers. It's hard to beat the old familiar acrostic that I learned as a child: Joy is Jesus first, others second, and yourself last. You can give without loving, but you can't love without giving.

As we focus on simplifying our lives, we will find that our beliefs become much simpler to live and to explain to others.

> At that time the disciples came to Jesus, saying, "Who then is greatest in the kingdom of heaven?" Then Jesus called a little child to Him, set him in the midst of them, and said, "Assuredly, I say to you, unless you are converted and become as little children, you will by no means enter the kingdom of heaven. Therefore whoever humbles himself as this little child is the greatest in the kingdom of heaven. Whoever receives one little child like this in My name receives Me (Matthew 18:1-4).

We may be tempted to think this admonition is for someone who is more spiritual than we are. If so, we must ask ourselves if we are willing to press on, or if we'll quit because it's too hard. Remember, it's sin that's hard. We will only be happy as we do what God calls us to do. If we try to run from Him, we'll end up like Jonah in the belly of the fish. I don't know about you, but being tossed by the waves to the point of nausea in a stinky place, having my skin bleached by stomach acid and my body entangled in seaweed, does not sound like something I would aspire to.

It doesn't matter what our flesh wants. Laziness does not bring prosperity or happiness. Our decision and the power to follow through on that decision, comes by walking in the power of the Spirit. As we determine to go God's way, no matter what, we need to get ready for total and dramatic change. Life as a disciple is not about rules; it's about relationship. To lighten our load we must turn to Jesus, give up control, and learn to trust. He's got the *super* and we've got the *natural.* The combination brings the *supernatural.*

Tabernacle Truth

As the priests entered the Holy Place of service and fellowship, they took no luggage with them. Let's try to keep our lives as simple and peaceful as possible, so that we will be more effective. Things can slow us down, if they don't have a specific purpose in our lives to lighten our load. Let's keep that in mind as we move forward on our journey.

Points to Ponder and Pray

Our *attitude* determines our *altitude*. "For where your treasure is, there your heart will be also" (Matthew 6:21). How deep do you want to go with God? What have you heard from the whisper of His still small voice as you read this chapter? What areas has He pinpointed that He wants you to simplify? In what ways would you like to see your life change in the giving of your time, talent, and treasure to further His Kingdom on earth?

Spend a few minutes talking personally with God and dealing with His promptings before you move on. Remember that it's a process, not a destination. Daily we must put off the old and put on the new as we renew our minds. The Lord desires that we "put off, concerning your former conduct, the old man which grows corrupt according to the deceitful lusts, and *be renewed in the spirit of your mind*, and that you put on the new man which was created according to God, in true righteousness and holiness" (Ephesians 4:22-24, emphasis mine).

You may find this prayer helpful to get you started:

Oh, Father, thank You for this primary place of service that You have carved out for me in my home and with my family. Thank You that You have given me everything I need in order to reflect Your light as I allow Your Spirit to fill and empower me. I make a covenant with you not to resist any of Your attempts to conform me to the likeness of Your Son. The moments of testing, the heat of that oven, will come when I put this book down, but these are some of the most exciting moments of anticipation. I will come to know the magnitude of all that You are! I may face great and immediate opposition, but Father, help me to look to the Lord Jesus and see the smile on His face as He says, "Don't be afraid, your enemies are already defeated. Walk with Me in victory." When I am under pressure by my family or friends, may I be more aware of the Lord Jesus saying, "If anyone would follow Me, he must be willing to forsake family and friends." May Jesus be exceedingly real in me, and may the supreme focus of my mind, heart, will, and life be His working out His real and living presence within me. The greatest desire of my life is what the Lord Jesus said: "Father, I have glorified your name on the earth, I have finished the work you gave me to do." I am in the midst of the work You gave me to do, and I want all the glory to go to You. Amen.

Chapter 14

Heritage of Prayer

On the morning of June 11, 1947, a phone rang in the kitchen of the Rishovd farmhouse in North Dakota. It was answered by the eldest grown daughter. “Eleanor,” a man’s voice said at the other end of the line, “your first niece was born this morning. We’ve named her Laurel Diane.” “Praise the Lord,” Eleanor exclaimed to her brother-in-law in Minnesota. “I will pray for her every day of her life!” That woman was my aunt, and I was the newborn she vowed to pray for. My mother’s older sister, Eleanor, did exactly that. And I have been truly blessed! The prayers and faithfulness of just one person can have an enormous impact.

I had the joy of being with my Aunt Eleanor in Santa Barbara, California, for the six days prior to her heavenly coronation in May of 1997. She gave me her wedding ring, which I wore for a year before passing it on to Trey for his engagement to his bride-to-be, as a reminder of our prayer heritage.

As I began doing Passionate Hearts conferences in 1995, I started wondering about my spiritual heritage on my father’s side. ” All I knew was that his mother, Hilda, had died when she was thirty-four years old. My dad was only three at the time. Imagine my surprise when a couple of weeks later I received a newspaper article in the mail from my dad dated March 11, 1925 - over 3/4 century ago. His cousin had recently had it translated into English from the original Norwegian. It read:

Mrs. Hilda Steen from St. Paul's Lutheran Church, Superior, Wisconsin, passed away early in the morning of February 21st. She had been ill only two weeks. She had to have a minor operation. She went to the hospital in the belief that in a few days she would be home with her family again. But the Lord made it happen in another way. He wanted to have her home with Himself. When she understood that the end was near, she called for her family to come to be near her. She said 'good-bye' to each of them. She asked them not to feel sad about what was happening because she was on her way to see Jesus. She praised her Savior, who had forgiven all her sins. She asked Rev. Torgerson to give her friends this message: "Take Jesus with you. It is such a great comfort." She was conscious right up to her death. She said several times, 'Wonderful Jesus. I am going home to Jesus.'

I grew up in northwestern Colorado with my parents and three brothers. I was born in Minnesota, but the family moved to Denver when I was three years old so that my dad could pursue his Master's degree at Denver University. After graduating he accepted a position as the high school science teacher in Meeker, Colorado, and that is where we lived until I graduated in 1965. My dad was also an excellent musician, carpenter, gardener and sportsman. In my eyes, there wasn't anything my dad couldn't do. He was my hero.

My mom was also an amazing person and a conscientious mother. She pursued her Bachelor's degree while I was a teenager and graduated from the University of Colorado when I was a junior in high school. She taught kindergarten for over twenty years, and went on to get her Master's degree when I was in college. She did a lot to help her kids get through college. She was also a diligent homemaker and an excellent Norwegian cook. Much of what I know in these areas, I learned under her tutelage.

Both my dad and mom were kind and caring parents who loved me and continually strived to provide their best for all four of their kids. I did not, however, grow up in a family of committed Christians. The church we attended weekly was a liberal mainline church where I rarely heard the name of Jesus Christ mentioned. It was after I left home for college, and my parents moved to Arizona, that they fully committed their lives to the Lord and began to grow as Christians.

This being the case, how can I explain that at the age of nine I heard how I could be forgiven for my sins and came to know Jesus Christ personally in a vacation Bible school across town from my own church?

How can I explain that I went to Bible camp for several summers, where that same message of my need for Christ was continually reaffirmed?

How can I explain that at the age of twelve I had a passionate desire to be a missionary?

How can I explain that in the eighth grade I wrote a paper for English class on my ambition to become a medical missionary?

How can I explain that I stayed morally pure throughout my teen years, even though I was running with the "in crowd," drinking, smoking, steeped in the party life, and dating guys who thought nothing of sleeping around?

How can I explain that at the age of eighteen God seized my heart at the same Bible camp I had attended years earlier, and redirected my entire focus in life?

The answer to all of these questions is *prayer*. I didn't know where I got the moral strength I needed. I just figured I had a strong will. But the Lord has shown me in subsequent years how weak my will really is. "The spirit indeed is willing, but the flesh is weak" (Matthew 26:41b, Mark 14:38b).

I never knew why I always prayed very simply, "Now I lay me down to sleep, I pray the Lord my soul to keep. If I should die before I wake, I pray the Lord my soul to take. Amen." When I was a teenager, my mother told me to pray that God would guide me to the right college and to the right husband—and I did.

Does God answer our prayers? Absolutely. How important is it, then, that we pray for ourselves and for those we love, putting prayer first on our list of priorities? Prayer is not the least we can do; it is the most. To attempt any work for God without prayer is as futile as trying to launch a space probe with a peashooter! We need more Christians for whom prayer is the first resort, rather than the last. When we give prayer a secondary place in our lives, we are making *God* secondary in our lives. We tend to get the jaundiced view that prayer enables us to do a greater work for God, rather than realize that prayer is, in itself, a greater work for God.

We often look upon prayer as a means of getting things for ourselves. The Bible's idea of prayer is that we may get to know God Himself. The value is not that He will hear us, but that we will hear Him. It's not monologue, but dialogue—God's voice in response to mine and vice versa. Listening to God's voice is the secret of the assurance that He will listen to mine.

Our prayers and God's mercy are like two buckets in a well. While the one ascends, the other descends. It's not so much submitting our needs to Him as submitting *ourselves* to Him. The self-sufficient *do not* pray, the self-satisfied *will not* pray, and the self-righteous *cannot* pray. In which category might you place yourself? If we would have God hear us when we pray, we must hear Him when He speaks.

Jim Elliot, a martyr for Christ at the hands of the Auca Indians in Ecuador, once said, "God is still on the throne, we're still on His footstool, and there's only a knee's distance between."

Samuel Chadwick said, "The one concern of the devil is to keep the saints from praying. He fears nothing from prayerless studies, prayerless work, or prayerless religion. He laughs at our toil, he mocks at our wisdom, but he trembles when we pray" (John Blanchard, *Gathered Gold*, Darlington, England: Evangelical Press, 1984). Most Christians are sadly unaware that God rules the world by the prayers of His saints.

After I committed my life to the Lord and headed off to a small Bible school in Michigan when I was eighteen, prayer began to take on a whole new flavor and dimension as I felt drawn by the Holy Spirit to my knees on many occasions. After a continued emphasis on prayer the following year at Biola University in California, my commitment to prayer with others became rather sporadic during the rest of my college years and well into my time of ministry and marriage. I began to subtly listen to the lie that I should get on with the important things in ministry and leave much of the praying to those who didn't feel called to an active ministry style.

It wasn't until we returned to the U.S. after almost a dozen years in Ireland that I felt a call from God to once again organize specific groups to pray with me, especially for my children. I have done this since 1987. After we moved to Orlando in the early '90s, God took me to the next level and impressed upon me to call others to pray beyond this primary area of the home.

My purpose here is not to give you a guideline of how I think you should pray. There are many books written from several perspectives that will encourage and help you. In the Passionate Hearts notebook you will also find prayer strategies and helps. (Ordering information in Appendix.)

One day the disciples came to Jesus and said, "Lord, teach us to pray" (Luke 11:1). It's significant that there is no record of the Lord teaching His disciples how to preach. But he took time to teach them how to pray and how not to pray. I hope you will follow their example and ask Him to teach you as well. As He does, you can adopt the Nike slogan, "Just do it"!

Tabernacle Truth

Let's go further into the sanctuary of the Tabernacle: the Holy Place. Once we *see* the light flickering on the walls and *feel* the warmth of its glow, *touch* the intricately carved gold rim of the table, and *taste* the Bread of Life who satisfies our hungry hearts, we begin to understand more of the absolute necessity of allowing the Holy Spirit to flow freely in our lives.

Now the pungent aroma filling the tent ignites other senses that draw us still nearer to the Holy of Holies. *Smell* the perfumed fragrance billowing from a gold object just in front of the veil, and *hear* the crackle of those burning embers below it.

The altar of incense is a symbol for us of intercession. "Therefore He is also able to save to the uttermost those who come to God through Him, since He always lives to make intercession for them" (Hebrews 7:25). We are the most Christlike when we intercede, because Jesus Christ our Savior lives to intercede for us.

The prophet Samuel said, "Far be it from me that I should sin against the Lord in ceasing to pray for you" (1 Samuel 12:23b). Have you ever considered that prayerlessness is a sin? Christ not only died for us, but also lives for us at the right hand of His Father right now. As we begin to live in this truth, how different will be our lives and the lives of those for whom we pray.

It is our joy and responsibility to intercede for others. The role of the high priest in Old Testament times was to offer sacrifice and to make intercession for others. His role of intercession was symbolized by his official garments. He wore the priestly ephod over his robe, which was like an apron, with two onyx stones, one fastened to each shoulder. On each stone were the names of six of the tribes of Israel. The breastplate was fastened to the ephod over the heart of the priest by gold chains, so it would never swing away from his heart. It had twelve jewels in four rows of three stones each. On each stone was engraved the name of one of the tribes.

Symbolically, every time the high priest entered the Tabernacle (and later the temple) to officiate in the presence of God, he bore on his shoulders, and close to his heart, the names of the tribes. This showed his responsibility and love for the people. In the same way, we are to carry a burden and a love for those whom God has placed in our lives.

Jesus Christ completed His sacrifice for our sins on the cross, but He continues even today to intercede for us. Every Christian is to partner with Him by interceding for others. Jesus continues His ministry today, as He has for 2,000 years, at the right hand of the Father. He is reigning by praying. As we follow Him, we too are to *reign with Him by praying.*

If we attend to God's business, He'll attend to ours. As we obey Him and do what He tells us to do, He will take care of what we are busily trying to do for ourselves. If we won't give up on Him, He won't give up on us. Remember that an excuse is a reason stuffed with a lie. Don't live in the past—move onward and upward. Prayer is not wrestling with God's reluctance to bless us; it is laying hold on His willingness to do so. Nothing lies outside the reach of prayer except that which lies outside the will of God. To pray effectively we must want what God wants. That, and that only, is to pray in the will of God.

Points to Ponder and Pray

Moses was a great leader, and yet I believe the children of Israel would have been wiped out and would never have reached the Promised Land (Israel) without his prayers of intercession. This is a life-and-death decision that we must make as well. Will we take our responsibility seriously to intercede for others, especially those nearest and dearest to us? The measure of our love for others can largely be determined by the frequency and earnestness of our prayers for them. We can leave our family and friends a great legacy of answered prayer, which will follow them all the days of their lives. This heritage of prayer is infinitely more important than an inheritance of wealth.

From our home base we can then move past our front door to our neighbors, church, workplace, city, state, nation, and the world. There is nothing that prevents us from having impact at any point on the globe twenty-four hours a day, seven days a week, three hundred sixty-five days a year.

The only thing that stands in my way is me. The only thing that stands in your way is you. What is your choice today? What commitment is God impressing on you to make in this incredibly important area of prayer?

Our second-born son, Jason, wrote a poem in 1996 when he was sixteen years old that I think beautifully lays this challenge before us. Please use this as your transition to your own prayer.

Waiting

Heads bowed in submission
Earnestly spoken words
Rising to the throne
Supplying Heaven's fragrance
As we make our requests known
Cleansing our lives
Through confession
And recognizing His powerful position
Thanking Him in advance
For the work He plans to accomplish
In our lives
Through His spirit
Empowering our efforts
Giving us strength to go the distance
Helping us to crush resistance
Reminding Satan that Jesus rose from the dead
Every time he rears his ugly head
Simple words are spoken
To the Lord of all
Heads bowed in submission
Waiting for His call.

Chapter 15

Revival Fires

I was breathless with excitement as I ran to the line outside the dining hall at the Grand Rapids School of the Bible and Music. I had just conducted my first evangelistic meeting with the street kids across from the school in the public park, where I had the joy of leading a few of these rough and wayward young boys to Christ. I had committed my life to Christ just a couple of months earlier. Even though I had a strong desire to share my faith with others, I was fearful of approaching adults because I had no confidence in my miniscule knowledge of the Bible. For this reason, I chose to speak to children and pass gospel tracts to adults.

I bubbled over with the exciting news that I had shared the gospel of Jesus Christ with young boys who seemed to have no direction in their lives. I stood in line behind Dave, who was the student body president and a senior who had grown up on the mission field and was preparing to be a missionary himself. Dave was tall and slender, and he looked down on me (in more ways than one). In the midst of my enthusiastic rendering of what had just transpired, Dave raised one eyebrow and seared me with an expression of utter disdain.

Needless to say, I felt foolish. "*Perhaps I should be more reserved now that I'm at Bible school,*" I thought to myself. *"I'm not sure I'm cut out to be here. I don't seem to fit the description of what a 'spiritual person' should be."* Deflated, I walked silently into the dining room.

A few days later, the student body gathered in the school auditorium for an evening chapel service. Dave was the designated leader for these times of worship and teaching. As he stood to address the students and faculty, he looked even more serious than usual. His lips trembled as he poured out a heartfelt confession of his cold and uncaring heart for the lost. He described the scene in the dinner line with me and proceeded to share how the Lord had pierced his heart as he walked away from there with a growing conviction of his sin of a prideful heart. As he poured out his confession and asked forgiveness from God, from me, and from the entire student body, I was transfixed. Sniffling and crying erupted from all corners of the auditorium as a steady stream of people stood to confess, in tears, the sin in their lives.

As we left there that night, the air seemed clearer, the night smells fresher, hearts lighter, and the joy contagious. I'll never forget Jack, a precious young man who had trouble walking and talking due to cerebral palsy as he moved unsteadily toward me with his arms outstretched for a big hug. From that day forward, Jack became one of my favorite friends. Others I knew began to move toward me with similar gestures of love, and when I graduated from GRSBM the following May, I left with tears of sadness. It had been the most amazing year of my life.

That evening chapel service was my first experience with corporate revival. Confession of sin and pride always precedes revival, and unity in the body of Christ is always a result. This is true whether it is unity between just two people, within a family, in a church, or to a city, state, or nation. Revival is the exchange of the "form of godliness" for living power. Every revival that ever came in the history of the world, or in the history of the church has put great emphasis on the holiness of God. As we begin to concern ourselves with the lack of holiness in our lives, rather than judging others, we release the power of God in our relationships and circumstances. Unless we are open to the work of the Spirit of God in our own lives, we will not see change, nor will God hear our prayers. In the book of Psalms, David says, "If I regard iniquity in my heart, the Lord will not hear" (66:18).

I experienced personal revival as an eighteen year old at Bible camp when I finally let Him take my life into His capable hands. At that point I understood what true freedom felt like. There have been many times, however, when I have temporarily lost that freedom because I allowed myself to become a captive of sin. Jesus said, "If you abide in My word, you are My disciples indeed. And you shall know the truth, and the truth shall make you free. Whoever commits sin is a slave of sin. If the Son makes you free, you shall be free indeed" (John 8:31b-32, 34b, 36).

Waiting for corporate revival is no excuse for not enjoying personal revival. In fact, personal revival is the predecessor of corporate revival. Revival comes through us to others as we allow ourselves to become channels. Paul admonished the Philippians:

> Fulfill my joy by being like-minded, having the same love, being of one accord, of one mind. Let nothing be done through selfish ambition or conceit, but in lowliness of mind let each esteem others better than himself. Let each of you look out not only for his own interests, but also for the interests of others (Philippians 2:2-4).

Paul goes on to lay out our model for this in the verses that follow. When Jesus humbled Himself and became obedient to the point of death, it was then that God highly exalted Him and gave Him the name that is above every name.

We are not promoted until *God* promotes us, and that comes as we humble ourselves. Is it any wonder that God is more willing to give revival than we are to receive it? Do not judge. Be humble before God and man. Humility comes before honor. If we continue to allow Satan to maintain a foothold in our lives, it will become a stronghold:

> "Be angry, and do not sin": do not let the sun go down on your wrath, nor give place to the devil. Let no corrupt word proceed out of your mouth, but what is good for necessary edification, that it may impart grace to the hearers. And do not grieve the Holy Spirit of God, by whom you were sealed for the day of redemption. Let all bitterness, wrath, anger, clamor, and evil speaking be put away from you, with all malice. And be kind to one another, tenderhearted, forgiving one another, even as God in Christ forgave you (Ephesians 4:26-27, 29-32).

When Tip and I went to Ireland in 1975, we found the western part of Ireland to be similar to what is described in the book of Acts—a frontier where the gospel had not yet penetrated. During our early years there, we saw the small camp of believers broaden and deepen, even with virtually no Bible-believing churches. The believers met from house to house, as they still do in many parts of the island.

As the years progressed, it became common for those of evangelical persuasion to worship together in peace with the charismatic believers. Each adopted the worship and prayer style they preferred, and no one judged anyone else for being different. What a wonderful, refreshing openness was in that body of Christ.

Just as God allows us to be different in worship style, temperament, heritage, gifting, color, race, and many other ways, we must allow the Holy Spirit of God to do a unique work in the lives of others without our interference. Sometimes that is very difficult, especially if we have a felt need to control people and circumstances. We must learn to be *grace givers,* full of grace *and* truth. It is not our responsibility to *change* people. It is our responsibility to *love* people — without conditions, expectations, or requirements.

We have much in common as believers, most notably the strong basis of our salvation in Jesus Christ. Why can we not major on the majors, minor on the minors, and join hands together in a lost and dark world that desperately needs the light we have? Division is why families are fragmented and why the church is often powerless in pulling down strongholds. We cannot bring down what we ourselves support. As long as we are divided, we cannot eliminate division. As long as we are distrustful, we cannot destroy unbelief. Until we humble ourselves, we will never remove pride.

Both a divided family and a divided church are unstable in all their ways:

> For though we walk in the flesh, we do not war according to the flesh. For the weapons of our warfare are not carnal but mighty in God for pulling down strongholds, casting down arguments and every high thing that exalts itself against the knowledge of God, bringing *every* thought into captivity to the obedience of Christ … (2 Corinthians 10:3-5, emphasis mine).

Jesus' parting prayer for us in John 17 shows the necessity of unity for the completion of God's work on earth. Christ's death reconciled us to Him *and* to one another, but we often present a pitiful demonstration of that truth to the world. If we can't even get beyond division within our own homes and churches, how can we export the message of reconciliation to the world? The church is divided racially, culturally, and socially. There are white-collar congregations, blue-collar congregations, and no-collar congregations. The church seems to be the only organization that can be out of business and yet stay in business.

We must agree to disagree without being disagreeable. Remember that kindness, gentleness, and meekness are the fruit of the Holy Spirit. In both our homes and our churches we must learn to accept that we can be united in Christ, even though we are different, and embrace those differences as a gift from God. A deep desire of my heart is to see the self-erected walls in families and churches crumble, so that we will learn to see beyond our differences to love each other unconditionally.

Tabernacle Truth

In the Tabernacle, directly behind the altar of incense, was the veil—the heavy partition of multicolored material and fine linen that separated the Holy Place from the Holy of Holies. The veil not only protected God's dwelling place from sinful man, but also protected the lives of those who weren't prepared to stand in His presence. The veil was ripped in half by God from top to bottom on the day Jesus' flesh was torn as He died on the cross to pay the penalty for our sins. From that day to this we have had unlimited access to the Holy of Holies with God.

There were two pieces of furniture in the Holy of Holies. The mercy seat with the two golden cherubim sat on top of the Ark of the Covenant: "And there I will meet with you, and I will speak with you from above the mercy seat" (Exodus 25:22a).

God always seeks us out before we find Him. Jesus said, "You did not choose Me, but I chose you and appointed you that you should go and bear fruit, and that your fruit should remain, that whatever you ask the Father in My name He may give you. These things I command you, that you love one another" (John 15:16-17).

I did not approach God about the Passionate Hearts ministry or about writing this book. He approached me. You did not approach God with the desire to read this book. He approached you. Paul, in his letter to the church at Philippi, writes, "Work out your own salvation with fear and trembling; for it is *God* who works in you both to will and to do for His good pleasure" (Philippians 2:12b-13, emphasis mine). First He causes us to want to do what He desires of us, and then He accomplishes it in us through His power. It's all about *Him*, not about *us*. All He wants is our trust, our faith, and our obedience.

There were three items in the Ark of the Covenant:

Aaron's rod—a shepherd's staff, which was a lifeless, dead stick that budded and blossomed. This is a symbol of the resurrection of Jesus Christ and the life that is reproduced in you and me to be His witnesses to others here on earth.

Pot of manna—a nutritious food that looked like frost, and was gathered off the ground six days a week by the Israelites as they wandered in the wilderness. This is a symbol of Jesus Christ—nourishment sent straight from God's arms to feed our hungry souls.

Ten commandments—the tablets of stone on which God wrote with his own hand and which were given to Moses on Mount Sinai. They provided a concrete standard of holiness for all generations. God says that some things are right and some things are wrong. Period.

When Moses came down from the mountain after fasting and praying for forty days, a change had taken place. His face shone so radiantly that he had to wear a veil to cover it. He was not aware of the marked change God's presence had made in him, but others were, because intimacy with God shows. The closer you are to the light, the more brightly it shines on you. The closer you get to God, the more clearly you see Him, and the more clearly you see yourself. It's impossible to be proud when you see yourself for who you really are. Do you want to be a real person rather than a hypocrite? You can trust God's Word that true intimacy with God precedes true humanity.

When we live out the truths of what we find in the Holy of Holies, we have the ingredients for both personal and corporate revival. As we experience resurrection life in Jesus Christ and share that life with others in obedience to His Word, we become life-givers as God reproduces His life in others. As we commune with Him from the mercy seat in that most Holy Place, we find ourselves walking intimately with our Creator.

The following is an old saying by an unknown author that gives a simple recipe for revival.

IF

If all the sleeping folk will wake up,
And all the lukewarm folk will fire up,
And all the dishonest folk will confess up,
And all the disgruntled folk will sweeten up,
And all the discouraged folk will cheer up,
And all the depressed folk will look up,
And all the estranged folk will make up,
And all the gossipers will shut up,
And all the dry bones will shake up,
And all the true soldiers will stand up,
And all the church members will pray up,
Then you can have a revival.

Points to Ponder and Pray

I pray that you won't put this book down until you have determined to be fully obedient to your Father in heaven. Remember that God's commands are *for* you, not against you, so that blessing will result. Once the fires of God have burned away the dross in your life, the pure fire of revival can be passed on to others. Without a life of obedience there is nothing of value to pass on to anyone.

Ronald Reagan once said, "I have long believed there was a divine plan which placed this land here to be found by people of a special kind, that we have a rendezvous with destiny. Yes, there is a spirit moving in this land and a hunger in the people for a spiritual revival. If the task I seek should be given to me, I would pray only that I could perform it in a way that would serve God." (Bob Phillips, *Phillips' Awesome Collection of Quips & Quotes,* Eugene, Oregon: Harvest House, 2001).

Can you echo this as a prayer from your own heart to the One who deeply longs to change you from within so that you can be used to ignite a spark in others? Please take all the time you need right now to listen to God and obey what He is saying to you.

Chapter 16

The Chosen Fast

As I opened my eyes and tried to shake off the groggy haze of awakening from a deep sleep, I realized that I was on the floor next to my bed. As I looked at my watch, I was horrified to realize that it was 10:00, and I'd already missed over two hours of classes.

When I transferred from a small Bible school in Michigan to Biola University in California, I had a deep desire to continue to grow in my love relationship with Jesus Christ. One of the ways God led me to do that was to invite everyone on my dorm floor to join me for prayer every weekday at 5:30 A.M. That morning, I had fallen asleep on my knees as I prayed, and my few stalwart friends who had joined me had stepped over my sleeping body to get out the door when they finished praying.

As the years went by, prayer became less a focal point of my life. It became just one more thing on my long "to do list." Subtly I listened to the lies of the evil one, believing that I needed to get on with the "important" things in ministry and leave the praying to those who didn't want to lead an active ministry style.

Satan is scared to death of the power we have at our disposal through prayer, and the first thing he wants us to do is get preoccupied with other things, even good things, that are the enemy of the best.

During my nineteenth year of life, I first heard about fasting from food for the purpose of seeking God more deeply in prayer. On an experimental basis I determined that I would fast for three days, drinking only water. I could see the campus cafeteria from my dorm room, and I honestly thought I was going to die of hunger that first day, as my stomach screamed for food. The second day was easier, and by the third day, I was convinced that I could go on indefinitely.

After that experience, however, I fasted very little until August of 1994, when Dr. Bill Bright, president of Campus Crusade for Christ, ended his first forty-day fast. It was then that God radically got my attention through a powerful message that he delivered that afternoon. The two things that God impressed me to do were to spread the nets wider and begin to fast one day a week. I began to do both immediately.

For many years thereafter I fasted a minimum of one day a week for at least forty weeks a year. Soon I was doing longer fasts, including four different types of forty-day fasts. I began to learn that fasting humbles me before God, helps me express love and worship to Him, curbs the flesh, helps me overcome temptation, and brings added discernment, direction, and power to my prayer life. My ministry was never the same from that point forward.

If you would be interested in reading about my first forty-day fast, you can read about it in Dr. Bill Bright's book, *The Transforming Power of Fasting and Prayer* (Orlando, FL: New Life Publications, 1997).

God expects us to fast, for both physical and spiritual reasons. Jesus didn't say *if* you fast, He said *when.* "Moreover, when you fast, do not be like the hypocrites, with a sad countenance...that they may appear to men to be fasting. Assuredly, I say to you, they have their reward. But you, when you fast, anoint your head and wash your face, so that you do not appear to men to be fasting, but to your Father who is in the secret place; and your Father who sees in secret will reward you openly" (Matthew 6:16-18).

As you look into a small book in the Old Testament, we find a man named Mordecai giving advice to Queen Esther. He said that if she remained silent about going before the king with a serious issue concerning the fate of her people, God would find someone else to do His bidding. He believed, however, that God had placed her there for a purpose.

> Do not think in your heart that you will escape in the king's palace any more than all the other Jews. For if you remain

> completely silent at this time, relief and deliverance will arise for the Jews from another place, but you and your father's house will perish. Yet who knows whether you have come to the kingdom for *such a time as this*" (Esther 4:13b-14, emphasis mine).

Esther's response was immediate. She called her nation to fast. "Go, gather all the Jews ... and fast for me; neither eat nor drink for three days, night or day. My maids and I will fast likewise. And so I will go to the king, which is against the law; and if I perish, I perish!" (4:16) Once that fast was finished, she brought her request before the king, found favor in his eyes, and ended up saving her entire nation.

Esther's response did not come out of a vacuum. It is clear earlier in the book that she disciplined herself to be obedient to the authorities in her life, and as a result God gave her respect from the people. When the call on her life was presented in God's perfect timing, she accepted His will and was confident that He would take care of her. As she actively mobilized those around her to fast and pray, she herself was an example and they responded by following what she modeled.

Esther presented herself in humility and obedience (5:1-6:14) and her influence reflected extraordinary power and authority for a woman in her time. That influence spread far and wide and continued into the generations after her death. In fact she wrote a decree that was entered in official records with full authority (9:29, 32).

My friend and author Dee Brestin found that, of those asked at women's retreats if they fast to strengthen their prayer life, 10% said regularly, 5% said occasionally, and 85% said rarely or never. In my Passionate Heart's conferences, an average of 57% of the women commit to fasting when clearly challenged.

Concerning our physical body, wise physicians confirm that giving the intestinal tract a day of rest by drinking only water has a cleansing, purifying effect on the body and gently forces it to utilize fat stores for energy. Fasting for a day flushes and reduces toxins built up on body systems, and decreases blood flow to the stomach while increasing blood flow to the brain. Just as we are commanded to give our bodies a day of rest after six days of work, it makes perfect sense to give our internal body a rest as well.

A type of fasting that I use frequently is mentioned throughout the

Bible during the reigns of Israel's kings: fasting throughout the day, but eating the evening meal. (See Judges 20:22-26 and 2 Samuel 1:1-12.) This is also the type that John Wesley and his followers used weekly.

This fast involves abstaining from all food and juice, but drinking plenty of water. Most importantly, it needs to be a time of seeking the Lord through prayer, Bible reading, and worshiping God. He is concerned with much more than our physical body. He wants to dig deeper and address the issues in our soul and spirit.

To fast simply for weight loss or for health reasons is to cater to the flesh and stop at the superficial physical level. It short-circuits the very goal God promises to bless in fasting, which is honoring Him. It may, however, have the secondary benefit of weight loss as it helps us break the bondage to food that often causes weight problems. The goal of weight control is to bring glory to God with our bodies. As we learn to honor God through the discipline of fasting it enables Him to honor us with self-control of body, soul, and spirit.

When fasting is accompanied by repentance from sin and it leads to change, it can be both useful and therapeutic. When it becomes an end in itself, however, it is sterile and counterproductive.

Spiritually, fasting increases the awareness of sin in our life and our need for repentance. It also gives us greater power for spiritual warfare, understanding of the needs of others, and a deeper sense of God's presence. I was amazed during my first forty-day fast to find there are about fifty verses on fasting in the Bible. Does this indicate to you, as it does to me, that God considers it very important?

Fasting is not something to boast about, but rather something we do with purpose and focus. We find Moses fasting for *intercession*, Elijah to *seek God*, Jesus for *power in ministry*, the people of Nineveh for *repentance*, Daniel for *revelation, intercession, and holiness*, Paul for *vision*, the Antioch Church for *direction*, Jehoshaphat for *overcoming the enemy*, David for *mourning* when he experienced the death of his child, and Ezra and Esther for *protection*.

Reasons for fasting are varied. In the book of Joel, when the nation of Israel was in deep peril, God said:

> "Turn to Me with all your heart,
> With fasting, with weeping, and with mourning."

So rend your heart, and not your garments;
Return to the Lord your God,
For He is gracious and merciful,
Slow to anger, and of great kindness;
Consecrate a fast (Joel 2:12b-13, 15b).

The most comprehensive chapter in the Bible regarding the discipline of fasting is Isaiah 58. If you would like to know more about "the chosen fast," the fasting that pleases God, I encourage you to read this chapter. The *ifs* and *thens* are stark as you consider *how* and *why* you should fast. I include some of it here.

"Is this not the fast that I have chosen;
To loose the bonds of wickedness,
To undo the heavy burdens,
To let the oppressed go free,
And that you break every yoke?" (6)

"*Then* your light shall break forth like the morning,
Your healing shall spring forth speedily,
And your righteousness shall go before you;
The glory of the Lord shall be your rear guard.
Then you shall call, and the Lord will answer;
You shall cry, and He will say, 'Here I am'"
(8-9a, emphasis mine).

"*If* you take away the yoke from your midst,
The pointing of the finger, and speaking wickedness,
If you extend your soul to the hungry
And satisfy the afflicted soul,
Then your light shall dawn in the darkness,
And your darkness shall be as the noonday.
The Lord will guide you continually,
And satisfy your soul in drought,
And strengthen your bones;
You shall be like a watered garden,
And like a spring of water, whose waters do not fail"
(9b-11, emphasis mine).

Behold, the Lord's hand is not shortened,
That it cannot save;
Nor His ear heavy,
That it cannot hear.
But your iniquities have separated you from your God;
And your sins have hidden His face from you,
So that He will not hear (59:1-2).

Jesus said, "Unless a grain of wheat falls into the ground and dies, it remains alone; but if it dies, it produces much grain. He who loves his life will lose it, and he who hates his life in this world will keep it for eternal life. If anyone serves Me, let him follow me; and where I am, there My servant will be also. If anyone serves Me, him My Father will honor " (John 12:24-26).

My life and ministry has radically changed since I sought to become obedient in this area, and yours will too. My only regret is that I didn't start sooner. It grieves me when I look back on all the years that I settled for less than God's best in my life and ministry.

Tabernacle Truth

When Moses went up into Mt. Sinai to receive the Ten Commandments from the hand of God, he fasted for forty days and nights. When he came down off the mountain to find the camp in a frenzied orgy and worshiping the golden calf, he threw the tablets to the ground and broke them in anger. At that point Moses had to go back up the mountain and fast for forty more days and nights before God gave him a "replacement set" of stone tablets. I must honestly say that I truly feel for poor Moses.

As Jesus was beginning His public ministry at the age of thirty, He went out into the desert to fast for forty days and nights. It's during this time that we read in the gospels that He was tempted of Satan to give it all up. Jesus rebuked Satan by quoting Scripture to him, and later admonishes us to follow His example. Could this extend even to undertaking a forty-day fast as we take on a new calling or ministry for the Lord?

Points to Ponder and Pray

Is the Lord prompting you to begin to obey Him in this area of fasting with your prayer life? How will you respond to His call? When will you begin? Please take the time right now to get your notebook and write your commitment with your signature and today's date. If you don't have a notebook handy, just jot it down at the bottom of this page. This is a commitment that you will always be grateful you made!

Chapter 17

The God of the Miraculous

Mrs. Killingsworth, you've been in labor all day and the baby hasn't moved down into the birth canal yet. If something doesn't happen quickly, we'll have to take the baby by Caesarian section."

It was April Fools' Day, 1977, in a small hospital on the west coast of Ireland, and there I was, in another "Red Sea" situation. Obstetrics had been my favorite specialty throughout my nursing training. I always loved the childbirth area because it was usually a place of great joy, rather than grief, suffering, and sadness. I'd never gotten over the miracle of new life coming into this world.

Finally, it was happening to me. After seven years of waiting and praying, the time had come. It was a Friday night, and our staff and students were having a College Life meeting, so Tip went to the phone to call them to prayer. Within an hour the baby began to move into place, and little Trey was born shortly after midnight. (Being the smart child that he is, he had no intention of being born on April Fools' Day.)

I have sometimes felt like a lightning rod for trouble, and yet as I have watched God's majestic hand weave the patchwork of my life, I am learning to trust that hand. With every problem He brings comes a purpose for building my faith and trust in Him and bringing me to a higher level. He is the only One who knows what niche I am to fill in life, so I must trust Him to shape me to fill it. Since only He knows what He has called me to do, I must trust Him to mold me in preparation for that.

Let me take you back a couple of years before my darling first-born son arrived.

In October 1975, when Tip and I had been married for nearly five years, God called us to serve with the campus ministry in Ireland. While we were there, I went to a doctor to determine why we were having no success in getting pregnant after trying for three years. The doctor discovered that I had a severely retroverted uterus and assured me I would never get pregnant without surgery. A specialist confirmed that diagnosis. At that time, I was ministering to students on the campus of University College Galway. I didn't want to even consider surgery until the school term ended in the spring, so Tip and I determined to pray that if God did not want me to have surgery, I would get pregnant before May. We enlisted the prayers of family and friends.

In February of 1976 we were ecstatic to discover that I was pregnant. When I told my doctor, he pointed toward the ceiling and said, "Somebody up there must be on your side."

After only three months we lost that baby through miscarriage. I remained in the hospital overnight, where I sank into a black pit of despair. But as the nurse flung open the drapes the following morning, I felt as though the arms of God came in with the sun and He wrapped me securely in His embrace. I can't explain how my darkness changed to joy in that instant, but that's exactly what happened. From that moment I had absolute confidence that God was still on His throne, and if He desired for us to have children, we would.

My doctors reconfirmed that surgery was imperative. The first pregnancy was a fluke, they believed, and certainly wouldn't happen again. But our faith had become solid and we made up our minds: no surgery. If God did it once He could certainly do it again. Well, He could, and He did.

A year later, in April 1977, I was in that same hospital in Galway, Ireland, with a beautiful eight-pound-twelve-ounce baby boy in my arms. When he was ten days old, we invited our friends and university students to pack into our home to dedicate Trey (Tipton III) to the Lord. Our text was First Samuel l:27-28, "For this child I prayed, and the Lord has granted me my petition which I asked of Him. Therefore I also have lent him to the Lord; as long as he lives he shall be lent to the Lord." One of the staff girls baked a beautiful cake with the following phrase written in icing: "Trey ... A Gift from God and to God."

Exactly five years to the day after God gave me supernatural peace in that hospital room following the loss of our first child, my four-year-old son got down on his knees and asked my Lord and Savior to become *his* Lord and Savior.

How can we *not* trust the incredible Master Designer of our lives? I always pray that my children will choose to love and serve their Creator God with singular passion. He is the God who hears and answers our prayers.

Trey is now twenty-four and a graduate of the University of Florida. God's hand has indeed been upon him. Tip and I thank God that we have been allowed to be a part of the process, but give Him all the glory for what He has done and is doing in Trey's life. To give you an idea of God's incredible faithfulness, allow me to share a few of the things the Lord has done in answer to this one prayer (plus twenty-four years of ongoing prayer for him).

Throughout high school and college Trey's first love was the Lord and His Word. He desired nothing more than to serve God with his life. He would be the first to admit that he was far from perfect, and yet God blessed him in amazing ways. One wall in our study is covered with memories of many of those blessings. What a joy it was to watch him throughout high school as he carried his Bible to school daily and became a spiritual leader on his campus and sports teams. He had a twelve-inch cross embroidered on the back of his letter jacket as a visual reminder to others that Jesus Christ held first place in his life. God gave him a great senior year on his football team, and after every touchdown he knelt in the end zone to thank the Lord. I believe that it was Trey's faithfulness to God that precipitated an offer of a place on the University of Florida, NCAA champion, Gator football team. God has given him many opportunities over the years to use his athletic platform for ministry.

On the way home from a mission trip to Ireland the summer after his freshman year at college, Trey knew God was calling him to a deeper level of commitment. As he began his sophomore year he fasted on Sundays and started revival prayer with a few friends at his house on Sunday afternoons. That group grew over the years, and they still gather to pray on Sunday evenings on campus.

Trey married his high school sweetheart, Jennifer Joy Lutz, on May 29, 1999. She fully committed her life to the Lord during college as a direct result of Trey's ministry. During her senior year she organized a prayer force of over 300 campus women and organized a Passionate Hearts conference at her college in Ohio, which I led. At that conference 70 percent of the young women in attendance indicated they had committed to Holy Spirit control, 79 percent to fasting with their prayer life, and 84 percent to ongoing prayer triplets. This was the direct result of serious concerted prayer by Jenny and her prayer team. Following her graduation, Jenny spent two years as a campus intern with Campus Crusade for Christ. When she gave birth to our first grandchild, Tipton Isaac, in August of 2000, Trey took over that internship for one more year.

As I share my story, it is my prayer that you will be challenged and encouraged to pass the torch to your own children as you seek to raise up a godly heritage. Before Trey left for college in 1995, I often went into his room at night to pray for him as he slept. My eyes filled with tears as I realized that my direct impact on his life was almost over. On his eighteenth birthday we gave him a public blessing and launched him into the world. It is yet to be seen what path his life will take. But as I have watched God's call on his life during his first twenty-four years, I am confident that he will continue to grow into a man of character and integrity whom God will use to further His kingdom on earth.

Those of you with children still living at home, let me assure you that these few short years God gives you with these precious gifts from Him will pass in the twinkling of an eye. Redeem every day that He gives you with them. Crawl into bed with your son or daughter for an intimate chat and prayer time before they go off to sleep at night. Even cautious, aloof, cocky kids lower their defenses in the quietness of their room. Pray with your children before they go to school, when they come home from school, before meals, before bedtime, whenever there is a problem.

Read Deuteronomy 6 for a brief rundown on how God commands parents to be on the job 24/7:

> You shall love the Lord your God with all your heart, with all your soul, and with all your strength. And these words which

> I command you today shall be in your heart. You shall teach them diligently to your children, and shall talk of them when you sit in your house, when you walk by the way, when you lie down, and when you rise up (4b-7).

That covers every part of our day and night. We have no time out.

Be continually vigilant to build that God-confidence in them that He is their Abba Father, their daddy. They can bring anything to Him to solve, from the tiniest details of life to the major faith tests.

Encourage your sons and daughters to be Daniels in this perverse generation. Don't shelter them from those God wants them to minister to as they grow, regardless of the educational approach you take.

Give them a chance to find their wings as you nourish and develop them from the nest. As you do all you can, draw from your Source of power daily on their behalf. Pray for them concertedly and regularly, with other moms whenever possible. If we don't pray for our children, *who will?*

We need to be models for our children in initiating and leading prayer, just as in every other area of their lives. I have always felt inadequate for the task and that I should have done more, but one way I did this was to challenge others to join us to pray for revival. As I prayed for Trey to begin revival prayer at UF, the Lord impressed me to organize an early-morning prayer gathering at University High School at 6:30 on Mondays for interested students, teachers, and parents. Our second son, Jason, was a senior and our third son, Josh, was a freshman that year. When Jason graduated, Josh continued to lead in this area.

I did the same with our girls, Trinity and Karis, who were seventh graders at the time. We went straight from the high school to Discovery Middle School at 7:30 every Monday morning. The girls grew from being very shy to becoming leaders in their eighth-grade year. When Josh was a senior and Trinity was a freshman, they prayed for a tithe of the 4,000 students at University High School for "See You at the Pole" that fall. That evening ABC news in Orlando quoted that 400 students were present! Does God answer prayer or what?

Trinity is now a leader in the same high school her older brothers graduated from. Because of her faithfulness God has allowed her to serve as junior class president and was re-elected as senior class president this year. She knows that God has given her this platform for ministry, not for self-promotion. I am so grateful for God's answers to prayer and that she continues to be faithful in ministry and shares her faith consistently with others. She took her spring break to participate in Spring Harvest 2001 at Daytona Beach, and just returned from two months with Teen Missions, including a month-long mission trip in Jamaica.

I have had at least one mom, often a group of moms, join me in my home for an hour of prayer regularly since 1987. When our family returned to the U.S. from Ireland in 1986 and were planted in Southern California, my fear for the spiritual future of my children nearly went off the charts. At the encouragement of Fern Nichols, a friend of mine and the founder of Moms In Touch, Int'l, I started my first little prayer group with only one other mom. That's all you need to start. I believe with all my heart this is one of the primary reasons my children have remained faithful to the Lord as they have gone through the public school system.

We need to saturate our lives with prayer. We must model the fact that we are convinced that prayer is the only way to live in obedience and intimacy with God. We are all busy, but we must cut back in other areas to live out our priorities in life. We will never regret the sacrifice.

I read about a woman named Monica who longed to see her son settle down with a godly wife. Instead he partied with his buddies, moved in with a girlfriend, and sired an illegitimate son. Monica begged her son to accept the life-changing truths of Christ, but instead he joined a cult and led others to join with him.

This young man eventually decided to move overseas, in part to escape his mother. But he hadn't reckoned with the power of her prayers that went with him, nor with his mother's perseverance.

Through the next fifteen years, Monica prayed for her son. She went to the local church twice a day to pour out her heart to God. She was so intense in prayer that her minister once sent her away, saying, "Go on home. As sure as you live, it is impossible for the son of a woman of such tears should perish."

She took those words as an encouragement from God Himself, and she never lost confidence that her prayers would one day be answered. Sure enough, the young man finally repented and gave his life to

Christ.

Who was that lost and sinful son? His name was Augustine—*St. Augustine*, the brilliant theologian whose passion for God and profound spiritual wisdom would one day come to shape the entire course of Western civilization.

Do I regret the emotional pain of waiting seven years for Trey's arrival into our family or of that first miscarriage? Not for one second. Are God's ways perfect? Always. Will we see the fruit in our lifetime? Not necessarily. Is it always safe to trust the Lord? Absolutely. Is it always easy? Absolutely not.

Sometimes I'm hesitant to tell stories like these because God doesn't always give the barren woman children, turn wayward children around, or cure people from cancer. But sometimes He does. In 1996 my mom had a mass on her liver that completely disappeared overnight as a result of prayer. Sometimes, despite intense prayer and fasting, He still says no or wait. We rejoice with those who rejoice and weep with those who weep. The bottom line is that we trust the God we love. He is God and we're not.

Tabernacle Truth

As we serve in the sanctuary at the golden Altar of Incense as the priests did daily in the Tabernacle, we begin to understand more fully how important it is that we pray. The coals that burned in that altar were taken directly from the blood soaked coals in the altar of sacrifice. It is through the intercession of Jesus Himself before the Father that we have the privilege to enter in and participate with Him. "But He, because He continues forever, has an unchangeable priesthood. Therefore He is also able to save to the uttermost those who come to God through Him, since *He always lives to make intercession for them* (Hebrews 7:25, emphasis mine).

"For we do not have a High Priest who cannot sympathize with our weaknesses, but was in all points tempted as we are, yet without sin. Let us therefore *come boldly to the throne of grace*, that we may obtain mercy and find grace to help in time of need" (Hebrews 4:15-16, emphasis mine).

It is not a magical transformation to become a person of prayer. It is accomplished moment by moment as we lift our thoughts and voices heavenward. I am far from where I want to be, and yet I know this is a journey, not a destination.

Miracles are meant to draw men to God. How big was the God of Moses? Big enough to part the Red Sea, bring water out of rocks, provide manna from heaven for food, and guide the Israelites with a cloud by day and a pillar of fire by night – just to name a few. This is the same God that we know and love. "Jesus Christ is the same yesterday, today, and forever" (Hebrews 18:8).

The miraculous is absolutely basic to Christianity. We rob Christianity of all excitement when we remove the miraculous. How big is *our* God?

Points to Ponder and Pray

Pray for those you love, regardless of what you see, or do not see, in their lives. Before you move on to the next chapter, will you make a commitment to pray for and with your loved ones on a consistent basis? Ask God for the strength you will need to be faithful. Perhaps He is directing you to connect with one or two other praying people to help you keep your commitment. As you ask Him for wisdom in how to move forward, He will be faithful to answer you. Just do it!

Chapter 18

You *are* the Sister!

"She's gone."

As I fought to shake off the grogginess of sleep, the words barely registered.

My husband repeated them with finality in his voice. "Karis is gone."

As my mind attempted to wrap itself around this unknown, my first thought was, "How could a perfectly healthy fourteen-year-old die in her sleep?" As I reached for my clock and realized it was 4:45 A.M., it began to dawn on me that our adopted daughter had run away from home sometime during the night.

A phone call from the mother of a new friend of Karis's had awakened Tip to relate that she heard a noise and got out of bed to see her daughter get into a dark-colored car and drive off into the night. When Tip went in to ask Karis if she knew anything about this, he found her bed empty and everything of value to her missing. It became clear in that moment that our daughter had no plans to return.

As dawn broke on that morning of August 1, 1998, we found ourselves filling out a missing person's report at our dining room table with a local sheriff. We'd had no inkling that anything was amiss, no warning to prepare us for this blow. Karis and our other fourteen-year-old daughter, Trinity, were both excited about entering high school in less than two weeks, and were in the middle of band camp in preparation for the fall football season. They had both been chosen to be in the Sapphires Color Guard with the band the previous May, and had been anticipating high school all that summer.

> "Count it all joy when you fall into various trials, knowing that the testing of your faith produces patience. But let patience have its perfect work, that you may be perfect and complete, lacking nothing. If any of you lacks wisdom, let him ask of God, who gives to all liberally and without reproach, and it will be given to him. But let him ask in faith, with no doubting, for he who doubts is like a wave of the sea driven and tossed by the wind. For let not that man suppose that he will receive anything from the Lord; he is a double-minded man, unstable in all his ways" (James 1:2-8).

The following sixteen hours comprised one of the severest trials in my life to that point, testing my ability to "run with endurance the race that is set before us, looking unto Jesus, the author and finisher of our faith" (Hebrews 12:1b-2a). Throughout that long day, and as the sun finally disappeared in the west and darkness settled in once again, I fought to keep my eyes on Jesus and off of my fears, as I prayed incessantly. There were several times that the anguish overflowed, as did the tears.

God's concern about our homes is not limited to a tent or bricks and mortar. After God gave us three active boys in four and a half years, there was a period of time that I thought this was surely enough. After our third son, Joshua, was getting close to his second birthday, I began to feel that strong desire to have another baby. Looking at my history of only brothers and sons, I fully expected a fourth boy.

Our three little guys took it upon themselves to pray every night for a baby sister. They had more faith on that than I did. Does it please the Lord to answer the prayers of His little ones? Absolutely. (Of course, being normal little boys, they regretted it many times over the years!) Their baby sister, Trinity Laurel, arrived on August 14, 1984, outweighing all of them at almost nine pounds. Needless to say, we were thrilled to have a daughter!

At thirty-seven years of age, with four children under the age of seven and a half, I definitely felt our family was complete. But from the time she could talk, Trinity began asking and praying for a sister.

To be honest, I didn't listen to her for one minute. I had absolutely no desire for a fifth child. My standard answer was, "Trinity, you *are* the sister". Since I, too, had grown up with three brothers, I knew she could survive it.

Well, you guessed it. The old "nudge" from the Holy Spirit returned when I was forty-six years old. One afternoon, as I drove Dee Brestin from the airport to a women's retreat in the Spring of 1993, she told me all about the Asian girl she and her husband had just adopted during their recent visit to Thailand. The Lord prompted me to begin seriously considering adopting a daughter. It was all I could think about throughout the weekend.

When I arrived home on Sunday evening, I broached the subject with Tip. Without missing a step he said, "Sure. Why not? There are a lot of children out there without a home. The Lord has given us a large home and a great family. What's one more?" God had obviously already prepared his heart.

From there I determined to talk with each of our four children separately, to be certain that none of them would be opposed to this idea. I painted the worst-case scenario so they could sift through some of the things that would change in our family, but I presented it as a family ministry opportunity. Without exception, each one was delighted at the prospect of expanding our family circle.

In the following weeks, as I began to check out overseas adoptions, I was stunned at the expense involved. It was clear that we could not afford this on our ministry living allowance, so we left this on the "back burner" and continued to pray.

One day shortly thereafter Tip arrived home and said he had talked with a woman in his office at Campus Crusade for Christ headquarters who had recently taken in two foster children from Boy's and Girl's Town.

My first response was negative. I knew the goal of the state was to get them back into their biological homes. I had no desire to be a revolving door, to bring a child into our home only to have him or her sent back into an abusive situation. God continued to put this on my heart, however, so I finally agreed to take the required parenting courses and be licensed by the state of Florida. After we finished the licensing process, in October of 1993, we only waited a few months before the phone rang with God's choice for our second daughter. At this point we had no idea that we would be allowed to adopt her a year later, but God knew.

My prayer throughout this process was fourfold:

1.) God would give us a daughter near Trinity's age. (Karis is six weeks older!)

2) She would come to know Jesus Christ as her personal Lord and Savior and that God would use her life. (She prayed with me to receive Christ on March 8, 1994, just two weeks after arriving into our home. In spite of her poor choices over the past three years there have been some bright moments of hope, and I still cling by faith to the hope that God will one day use her in the harvest with others who have also had a difficult path in life.)

3) She would have a joyful, happy personality and not bring anger and hostility into our home. (She has a sanguine, sunny temperament and is a joy to be around when she is walking with God.)

4) She would not have sexual abuse in her background. (To our knowledge, this is the case.)

Keisha, the sister Trinity prayed for, arrived in our home in February of 1994, a nine-year-old African-American girl from Orlando. She was born Stephanie Lashawn Brown, and had been in and out of foster homes since the age of one. When she was six years old she was adopted by a single woman, and her name was changed to Keisha Odessa Davis. After a couple of years, this woman had to sign off on her parental rights due to abuse.

As we were preparing to adopt Keisha, I called her into my bedroom one day to tell her some stories from the Bible where God changed people's names to signify a changed life. I asked her if she would like to have a new name, and she was delighted at the prospect.

When the adoption went through in April 1995, she became Karis Love Killingsworth (God's grace and love). During her first six months with us, her desires began to change, from becoming Whitney Houston II and singing in Hollywood, to being a missionary to children in Albania. It was easy to see that God was at work in her life.

I wish that had been the end of her struggles and wrong choices, but it wasn't. In three years she ran away nine times, the most recent being just last month. The time between each escape has become less, and the time away has become longer. We have tried a number of things to help turn her around, including home schooling her for a year. When she was fifteen, we sent her to Phoenix, Arizona, to live with my brother and his family. After eight months of success, she fell back into her old patterns, and was returned to us on her sixteenth birthday.

Karis is now seventeen and has violated a six-month probation for shoplifting. Every time she comes home she is very repentant, but has not grown to the place where she can handle the strong temptation to do her own thing. Only God knows her future, but it is my responsibility as her mother to continue to pray for her, regardless of how dark the circumstances may appear.

Have I despaired of Karis ever repenting and turning her life around? Yes. Will I give up or give in? Not as long as God gives me the breath to pray for her. Is God on my timetable? No. Is He faithful to hear my prayers, and answer according to His will? Absolutely. Will I live to see God use my daughter greatly in the lives of others? Only God knows.

We continue to pray daily that Karis will become a committed woman of God, that she will follow Him with her whole heart, and that He will use all the negative things in her life to bring glory to her Father in heaven.

If we had it to do over again, knowing what we know now, would we make the same decision to bring Karis into our family? Without a doubt. I love that precious young lady with all my heart.

I would encourage you with all my heart to keep your spirits attuned to the leading of the Lord in the area of valuing children. Often we make our decisions concerning what is important in life according to the world's standards rather than God's. A good place to start is Psalm 127 and 128.

> "Unless the Lord builds the house,
> They labor in vain who build it;
> Unless the Lord guards the city,
> The watchman stays awake in vain.
> It is vain for you to rise up early,
> To sit up late,
> To eat the bread of sorrows;

For so He gives His beloved sleep.

Behold, children are a heritage from the Lord,
The fruit of the womb is a reward.
Like arrows in the hand of a warrior,
So are the children of one's youth.
Happy is the man who has his quiver full of them;
They shall not be ashamed,
But shall speak with their enemies in the gate.

Blessed is every one who fears the Lord,
Who walks in His ways.
When you eat the labor of your hands,
You shall be happy, and it shall be well with you.
Your wife shall be like a fruitful vine
In the very heart of your house,
Your children like olive plants
All around your table.
Behold, thus shall the man be blessed
Who fears the Lord."

Perhaps God desires for you to open your home and heart to a child who needs a family. If every Christian family did this, there would be no homeless children. Remember that what God orders, He can pay for. Don't use your low income or busy life as an excuse. God wants us to trust Him. Our adoption didn't cost us a penny. God answers prayer, and one way or another, He *will* provide.

Once we are married, our ministry as women is to be focused on our families first, as depicted so beautifully in Proverbs 31. But it's not to stop there. That chapter goes on to show how our lives are to radiate with concentric circles into our neighborhoods, churches, work places, cities, and out into the world at large. Regardless of our age or season of life, *all* of us have the privilege of impacting even the furthest point on the globe twenty-four hours a day through prayer.

When Karis first ran away on August 1, 1998, I had no idea where she was, but God knew. Despite the comfort of that knowledge, fear tore at my heart for her safety and protection, and feelings of guilt swept over me. As I returned from a long prayer walk that night, my eyes still damp with tears, Tip met me at the door with the joyful news, "She's been found!"

The story of the lost sheep in Matthew 18 suddenly became more than a parable to me. It became a reality.

> "Take heed that you do not despise one of these little ones, for I say to you that in heaven their angels always see the face of My Father who is in heaven. For the Son of Man has come to save that which was lost. What do you think? If a man has a hundred sheep, and one of them goes astray, does he not leave the ninety-nine and go to the mountains to seek the one that is straying? And if he should find it, assuredly, I say to you, he rejoices more over that sheep than over the ninety-nine that did not go astray. Even so it is not the will of your Father who is in heaven that one of these little ones should perish" (10-14).

As we drove to pick her up, I knew what God wanted me to do. When I saw my "little lost lamb" sitting on the curb looking at the ground, I got out of the car and ran over to her, pulled her to her feet, and wrapped my arms around her. There was much work ahead of us, and it isn't over yet, but that moment was a time to rejoice!

Tabernacle Truth

As we fellowship with others in the Holy Place, our primary place of service is usually in or from our homes. For many of us, children and grandchildren make up an integral part of that home. As we share the light and the bread with those God gives us within our homes, He will broaden our vistas to those around us.

We all need a companion in our "desert," but more than that, we need a Shepherd. Without the guidance of God's Spirit we become hopelessly lost. Pride in our own knowledge of the desert is deadly. If we are rebellious, we cannot operate within His framework of wisdom, knowledge, thought, or direction. We will never rise to a strong spiritual level unless we allow ourselves to be conformed to His Spirit.

Most of the Israelites tried to avoid discipline by either God or Moses. We, too, often choose paths that are easy for us. In the 23rd

Psalm, David noted that the rod and staff of the shepherd *comforted* him. But there is so much more in our relationship with the Lord than discipline, just as should be the case with our own children. This is that Psalm with an added emphasis for clarity. Face it. The Lord is crazy about you!

The Lord is my Shepherd: that's ***relationship***.
I shall not want: that's ***supply***.
He makes me to lie down in green pastures: that's ***rest.***
He leads me beside the still waters: that's ***refreshment.***
He restores my soul: that's ***healing.***
He leads me in the paths of righteousness: that's ***guidance.***
For His name's sake: that's ***purpose.***
Yea, though I walk through the valley of the shadow of death: that's ***testing.***
I will fear no evil: that's ***faithfulness.***
For You are with me: that's ***protection.***
Your rod and Your staff, they comfort me: that's ***discipline.***
You prepare a table before me in the presence of my enemies: that's ***hope.***
You anoint my head with oil: that's ***consecration.***
My cup runs over: that's ***abundance.***
Surely goodness and mercy shall follow me all the days of my life: that's ***blessing.***
And I will dwell in the house of the Lord: that's ***security.***
Forever: that's ***eternity.***

The writer of Hebrews also emphasizes the loving motives behind God's correction as he quotes from Proverbs 3:11-12.

"My son, do not despise the chastening of the Lord,
Nor be discouraged when you are rebuked by Him;
For whom the Lord loves He chastens,
And scourges every son whom He receives" (Hebrews 12:6).

Discipline yields fruit over time. "Now no chastening seems to be joyful for the present, but painful; nevertheless, afterward *it yields the peaceable fruit of righteousness to those who have been trained by it*"

(Hebrews 12:11, emphasis mine).

In our home we daily pray the prayer found in First Chronicles 4:10. Perhaps you would like to make that a practice in your home as well.

Prayer of Jabez

"Oh, that you would bless me indeed,
and enlarge my territory,
that Your hand would be with me,
and that You would keep me from evil,
that I may not cause pain!"

Points to Ponder and Pray

I recently found a story on the Internet that grabbed my heart. It is my prayer that as you read this, you would ask God to speak to you about how you should personally apply it in your own life and family.

One day a young man was standing in the middle of town proclaiming that he had the most beautiful heart in the whole valley. A large crowd gathered and they all admired his heart for it was perfect. There was not a mark or a flaw in it.

Yes, they all agreed it truly was the most beautiful heart they had ever seen. The young man was very proud and boasted more loudly about his beautiful heart. Suddenly, an old man appeared at the front of the crowd and said, "Why your heart is not nearly as beautiful as mine." The crowd and the young man looked at the old man's heart. It was beating strongly, but full of scars, it had places where pieces had been removed and other pieces put in, but they didn't fit quite right and there were several jagged edges. In fact, in some places there were deep gouges where whole pieces were missing.

The people stared — how can he say his heart is more beautiful, they thought? The young man looked at the old man's heart and saw its state and laughed. "You must be joking," he said. "Compare your heart with mine, mine is perfect and yours is a mess of scars and tears."

"Yes," said the old man, "yours is perfect looking but I would never trade with you. You see, every scar represents a person to whom I have given my love - I tear out a piece of my heart and give it to them, and often they give me a piece of their heart which fits into the empty place in my heart, but because the pieces aren't exact, I have some rough edges, which I cherish, because they remind me of the love we shared. Sometimes I have given pieces of my heart away, and the other person hasn't returned a piece of his heart to me. These are the empty gouges — giving love is taking a chance. Although these gouges are painful, they stay open, reminding me of the love I have for these people too, and I hope someday they may return and fill the space I have waiting. So now do you see what true beauty is?"

The young man stood silently with tears running down his cheeks. He walked up to the old man, reached into his perfect young and beautiful heart, and ripped a piece out. He offered it to the old man with trembling hands. The old man took his offering, placed it in his heart and then took a piece from his old scarred heart and placed it in the wound in the young man's heart. It fit, but not perfectly, as there were some jagged edges. The young man looked at his heart, not perfect anymore but more beautiful than ever, since love from the old man's heart flowed into his. They embraced and walked away side by side.

Author Unknown

Is there someone to whom you need to give a piece of your heart? Are there people in your own family who are far from the Lord? Have you relinquished them into God's capable hands? Do you pray in faith for them daily? Is He saying something to you about your value system regarding children and family? Listen to His voice and obey Him.

When you experience discouragement with fatigue, frustration, failure, or fear, remember what the prophet Nehemiah said to the people. "Do not be afraid of them. *Remember* the Lord, great and awesome, and fight for your brethren, your sons, your daughters, your wives, and your houses" (Nehemiah 4:14b, emphasis mine).

Remember the Lord and His blessings. List them from both the past and the present, and practice His presence in the future. "Whatever things are true, whatever things are noble, whatever things are just, whatever things are pure, whatever things are lovely, whatever things are of good report, if there is any virtue and if there is anything praiseworthy—*meditate on these things.* The things which you learned and received and heard and saw in me, *these do, and the God of peace will be with you*" (Philippians 4:8-9, emphasis mine).

These were the five daily themes that we used in our Backyard Bible Club a few years ago. You may want to memorize them because they are the "bottom line" for both you and your children.

> Little sins grow into big sins and big sins kill.
> Give God a call and He will save you from a fall.
> What you feed grows and what you starve dies.
> You will end up with the most when you learn to stay close.
> Don't trade away the things that don't fade away.

Chapter 19

The God of Dreams and Visions

I awoke in a sweat, my heart pounding. Looking around in the semi-darkness, I remembered that I was in the Military Hotel in Moscow, Russia. It was March 25, 1994, and I was on a mission trip sharing Christ in the universities there. Glancing at my watch, my mind came to full alert. It was 4:00 A.M. and I had just had an incredibly powerful dream. I didn't want to be mystical about it, and yet I felt I had heard from God. It was an intricate and detailed story, but the bottom line was that I was to call people everywhere and from every walk of life to pray, regardless of their response.

I had no idea what this dream meant or how to implement it, so I continued to do what I was already doing. From that point, though, it was as if a countdown clock began to tick. I had been hosting groups of moms in my home weekly for the previous eight years to pray for our children, and I had seen God's incredible faithfulness on behalf of my brood. Their lives were an ongoing saga of answered prayer and divine encounters. They were far from perfect (they take after their mom!), but they continued to walk with Him in the middle of "Babylon," which for them was the public school system.

Since I took on the job of national field coordinator with the Mothers Who Care ministry shortly after settling in Orlando, God had been gradually enlarging and expanding my vision for calling women to prayer. Was this something different? If this was from God, He would certainly clarify what He meant by that dream.

In August, Tip and I were asked to sing for Dr. Bright's praise gathering to celebrate the conclusion of his first forty-day fast. If we hadn't been singing, I wouldn't have gone, since all five of our children were preparing to start school a few days later. But on that day God spoke to me again. The message came through that I was to spread the nets wider and begin to fast one day a week.

In early December, when Dr. Bright felt God impressing him to invite the religious leaders of America to Orlando for "A Special Call to Prayer and Fasting," the Lord nudged me to attend. Dr. Bright and our dear friend Steve Douglass encouraged me to work at the conference. Nancy Wilson, the associate director of the Student Venture ministry, began to pursue me as a prayer partner, and challenged me to attend the "Something's Happening USA" prayer conference for high school students in Minneapolis after Christmas.

After praying about it, I felt God's leading to attend the conference. God gave me a deep desire to explore ways to develop a conference of my own to bring women into intimacy with God, and to teach them how to become women of power, purity, and prayer.

Throughout those four days and nights, my mind and heart were filled with illumination from the Holy Spirit. I spent the entire time listening to God, writing, and praying. When I returned to Orlando, I committed to an extended fast (twelve days) to make absolutely certain I was hearing the Lord correctly. This turned out to be the ninth month of a "gestation period," for a new ministry was about to be born.

My journal entry on January 1, 1995, reads:

> *Jesus, as I begin this time of travail, I have a sense of foreboding, struggle, weakness … yet a strong hope for the special ways that You are going to speak to me, show me, comfort me, grow me, love me, and bless me as I seek Your face, Your will, and Your guidance for the future. I so want JOY for the journey, all who seek will find, pardon and freedom in every area for those who obey. I am counting the cost as never before. The time is short and I MUST obey Your voice in EVERY area and trust You to show me, regardless of what others may think or say. I love You, precious Father. Thank You for loving me with an everlasting love. Open my eyes. … Laurie.*

January 9:

> *My Lord and my God, it's now the ninth day of my fast and I strongly sense the moving and speaking of Your Spirit over the past weeks. After spending 6 hours yesterday at the computer on my proposal, I feel that I've covered every area that You have shown me. Don't let me make a mistake concerning Your direction and counsel, Lord. Give me the strength and confirmation for what You want me to do. I feel like Gideon in Judges 6. Why me, Lord? Is this really You, Lord? Prove it! Make it clear. I want to feel Your touch, Your power, Your fire, Your passion! I love you. ... Laurie.*

As I came off that fast, I went to Colorado Springs for the National Day of Prayer Coordinators Conference, and there the remainder of the strategy for the concerts of prayer fell into place. Shirley Dobson was warmly supportive and encouraging as I shared my vision with her.

The birth of this vision came to pass a few weeks later. In a women's retreat in Melbourne Beach, Passionate Hearts was born. A lot of refining has gone on since that faltering start, but the format is basically the same. The conference is divided into three sessions: "Women of Power" followed by a personal prayer workshop on repentance, "Women of Purity" followed by a prayer workshop for the family, and "Women of Prayer" followed by a prayer workshop for our nation and the world.

God's confirmation and direction was overwhelming that first weekend as 26 percent prayed to receive Christ, 72 percent committed to Holy Spirit control, and 85 percent committed to ongoing prayer triplets. Tears flowed freely all weekend. God's deep work in women's lives has been a characteristic of every conference through the years.

Even though each conference has a personality of its own, no matter what the denomination, the statistics haven't varied much since that first "maiden voyage." On average, based on the Praise Reports turned in at the end of each conference, about 20 percent trust Jesus Christ as their Savior, 60 percent commit to Holy Spirit control and to fasting with their prayer life, and 70 percent commit to ongoing prayer triplets.

To be honest, it would take an entire book to describe all that God has been teaching me. It's an ongoing choice to pick up my cross daily and follow Him. I would, however, like to give you a few nuggets to consider and pray about as you move forward with God toward the dream He is putting in your heart.

When God gives us a vision of what He wants us to do, He then takes us down into the valley to chisel us into the shape of the vision. It's in the valley that we often give up, or at least want to give up. Until that vision is made real in us, Satan has a heyday with us in his attempts to defeat us before we get off the mark. It's interesting that we are the only ones who seem to be in a hurry. God has all the time in the world, and His goal is to test our mettle to see if He can trust us.

We are to be a living sacrifice to God. The problem is, we keep crawling off the altar. The Bible says we are to "present your bodies a living sacrifice, holy, acceptable to God, which is your reasonable service. And do not be conformed to this world, but be transformed by the renewing of your mind, that you may prove what is that good and acceptable and perfect will of God" (Romans 12:1b-2). Notice that He wants to *transform* us, not *translate* us. He left us here for a reason and has already prepared the good works in which He wants us to walk. "For we are His workmanship, created in Christ Jesus for good works, which God prepared beforehand that we should walk in them" (Ephesians 2:10).

We think we know better than God does and attempt to shape ourselves. If we allow Him to put us on His potter's wheel and whirl us around as He presses His fingers in just the right places, we will become exactly what He desires us to be to fulfill the vision He has for us. What we put on the wheel always comes back around until it is perfected in His hands. We can delay that by resisting, or obey and reap the harvest of joy that awaits us. This is the only place we will ever be satisfied. We can try everything else in the book and come up empty. God will never let us be satisfied with less than His perfect plan for our lives because He loves us.

God does not usually tell us ahead of time where He is leading us. The only thing He shows us consistently is Himself. Our priorities must be God first, God second, and God third, until our life is faced steadily with God, and no one or nothing else matters anymore. Keep paying the price. Let God see that you are willing to live up to the vision He gives you.

> Create in me a clean heart, O God,
> And renew a steadfast spirit within me.
> Do not cast me away from Your presence,
> And do not take Your Holy Spirit from me.
> Restore to me the joy of Your salvation,
> And uphold me by Your generous Spirit.
> Then I will teach transgressors Your ways,
> And sinners shall be converted to You (Psalm 51:10-13).

Remember in all this that you need to "chill out" in order to hear the voice of God clearly. If you rush in where angels fear to tread, you will feel more stress, lose your joy, become less productive, and become unable to hear God. You will need to stop the constant push of a hurried lifestyle, learn to say no, obey the fourth commandment to take a day off weekly to focus on the Lord, and wait for His timing.

> "Do not remember the former things,
> Nor consider the things of old.
> Behold, I will do a new thing,
> Now it shall spring forth;
> Shall you not know it?
> I will even make a road in the wilderness
> And rivers in the desert" (Isaiah 43:18-19).

Martin Luther King's most famous and remembered words are "I have a dream." He also said, "If a man hasn't discovered something that he will die for, he isn't fit to live." (John Bartlett, *Bartlett's Familiar* Quotations, Boston, MA: Little, Brown and Company, published continuously since 1863). Those are strong words, and yet we need to be put on notice that God created us for a purpose. As we humble ourselves with a pure heart before our Creator God, He makes that purpose known to us. Satan fights the birth of anything, but God is more powerful than Satan and dwells within us.

The making of a man or woman of God takes longer than anticipated, costs more than we want to pay, and takes us through more trouble than we thought we could manage. But the Bible is clear from start to finish that if we give Him all we have, He will take care of us. There is a wonderful story tucked away in First Kings 17:8-16 that clearly teaches this principle. As the poor widow obediently gave the prophet Elijah all she had, fully expecting that she and her son would die as a result, God stepped in with a miracle. It didn't happen before she obeyed, but *after*. Even though there was famine and drought in the land, God saw to it that her bin of flour was not used up, nor her jar of oil empty, until the day God sent rain on the earth. Will we step out in faith, even if we're "baby-steppin' it"? Let's go for it!

Tabernacle Truth

During the years in the wilderness the unfaithful children of Israel perished and God raised up a brand new generation. They had never known the pleasures of Egypt and were able to identify more closely with the Lord, beginning to see things from His perspective. This time, when the call came to cross the Jordan and go in to possess the land which had been promised to Abraham, the majority of them were ready to obey. After forty years in the desert the Lord passed the leadership from Moses to Joshua, and it was he who led God's people across the Jordan River and into the Promised Land.

The Lord continued to expect active participation, courage, and obedience from Joshua and the people. As at the Red Sea, God performed the miracle. This time He waited until those carrying the Ark Of The Covenant stepped from dry land into the raging currents of the Jordan River. In contrast to the Red Sea crossing, the people were to follow far enough behind the ark so that every person in that huge group of millions could *see* it. The ark, carried by the priests and Levites, *was their guide*. When it moved, they moved. (If you would like to read this entire story, you will find it in Joshua, chapters three and four.)

"When you see the Ark Of The Covenant of the Lord your God, and the priests, the Levites, bearing it, then you shall set out from your place and go after it" (Joshua 3:3). The ark was the vessel through which God communicated to His people and where He manifested His glory. It also represented the coming Messiah who would be the living revelation of God's glory. Jesus Christ is the One we look to under the new covenant to guide us into our promised abundant life.

After Joshua told the people where to look for guidance on their journey he gave them another command, "Sanctify yourselves, for tomorrow the Lord will do wonders among you" (Joshua 3:5). Joshua knew that God is holy and would not tolerate any unclean thing in His presence. We are cleansed from all sin at the moment of our salvation (Red Sea crossing), but an intimate Christian walk requires a daily cleansing.

As with the Israelites, we cannot see the glory of God until we have been cleansed, first at our "Red Sea" salvation experience and later, in preparation for crossing our "Jordan." Only then can we hope to see the miracle of God. Once we see the ark — Jesus — our eyes are never to lose sight of Him. When God says to move we must move, not before and not later, but then.

Early the next morning the people were straining their eyes to see the ark, watching and waiting expectantly to see what God would do. As the ark began to move toward the river, God performed His promised miracle. The mighty power of the living God rolled the waters back. They rose up in a heap, exposing firm, dry ground so His people could pass over into the land of promise. Our God has not changed. He still rewards faithful obedience with miracles.

Think of the awesome joy the people must have experienced as they passed the spot where the priests and Levites stood holding the ark. Each one knew that God – their God – was real. After forty long years in the wilderness, the land of milk and honey was theirs to conquer.

Prior to the crossing of the Jordan there was *conflict resulting in defeat*. After the crossing there was *conflict resulting in victory*. The forty years in the wilderness had brought great change in their relationship with God. They were now ready to submit to the will of the Lord and respond eagerly to His call.

Points to Ponder and Pray

We can either be pitiful or powerful, but not both. The minute we start dreading something, we lose our power. Which will we choose?

Has God given you a dream for your future? Has He planted a deep desire and a passion in your heart that you just can't shake? Please stop here to take a moment with the Lord to formulate a plan for what He has laid on your heart to do. God created you for a purpose and He has gifted you uniquely to carry out that purpose.

Resolve in your heart before the Lord that you will use all the resources He gives you to accomplish what He has set before you. Use it or lose it (Matthew 25:14-30). God has given you the indwelling Spirit of God to flesh out His will for your life, but you must work out your own salvation with fear and trembling. He won't just drop it out of heaven into your lap. No, it won't be easy, but remember that you will *grow up* in the places that you don't *give up*. Never forget that responsibility is your response to *His* ability.

It will be worth it all when we see Jesus. He won't deliver us from the obstacles and trials, but will take us through them. The only way out is through.

Perhaps He has already spoken to you about the next faith challenge He has in mind for you. If He hasn't, just ask Him!

Chapter 20

It's Harvest Time

It's harvest time! One warm December day in 1998, as I stood alone in the middle of Gomorrah near the Dead Sea in Israel, I was struck by a fresh awareness that harvest involves a chain of miracles. I was overwhelmed by the awesome power and might of our God—not because it was a beautiful, lush garden of paradise; in fact, it was the antithesis of that. This was not fruitfulness, but barrenness. There was not one blade of grass or living creature as far as I could see to the north, south, east, or west. Very few people are even aware that this wasteland still stands today, as a monument to the certainty of God and His Word.

The Bible indicates that this land was once like a garden of the Lord in Genesis 13:10. When Abraham gave Lot the first choice of the land, this area is what he chose. "And Lot lifted his eyes and saw all the plain of Jordan, that it was well watered everywhere (before the Lord destroyed Sodom and Gomorrah) like the garden of the Lord." Today that western side of the Dead Sea is an ugly, barren land. There is nothing beautiful about it. It's a true sign of God's judgment, not His blessing.

I climbed as high as I could on what were once buildings in a thriving metropolis, but now stand like giant sand dunes. As I neared the top I was fearful that I'd fall, so I began to carefully back down one of those steep slopes. With my video camera slung over my back, I prayed that God would show me the evidence that I'd heard a few others had found here. Evidence of brimstone (hailstones of sulfur) that fell from the sky one day thousands of years ago, because the people rejected the warning of a holy God to turn away from their lives of sin and turn in repentance to Him. Because they refused, their entire city was incinerated, burned down to the bedrock. This was the same God who promised great blessing for obedience.

About halfway down I noticed reddish marks in the ashy sand, so I leaned forward to dig with my fingers to see what was underneath. As I brushed away the loose ash and sand, I pulled out what looked like an oyster shell with a pearl inside. My heart began to race! As brimstone hits the earth and ignites, it burns until it is completely enveloped with whatever it is burning, and the fire is snuffed out for lack of oxygen. As I began to fill a plastic bag with these treasures, it was almost as if God was saying, "Laurie, warn the people. These are not just children's Bible stories. This is history. I am God and I am true to My Word. I will be returning soon for my Bride, the church. Will she be ready for my return and the wedding feast of the Lamb?"

As I surveyed Gomorrah from that high vantage point, the last thing that came to mind was harvest. Just as the miracle of life in a seed is released through the creative order of God, so the ministry of winning lost souls cannot be done by the efforts of men and women alone, but in doing things God's way. "So then neither he who plants is anything, nor he who waters, but God who gives the increase" (1 Corinthians 3:7).

Harvest comes through prayer, for it's God who brings the harvest. The harvest can and must be prayed in. History confirms that evangelism alone rarely produces spiritual awakening. Rather, *prayer* produces the awakening, and this awakening inevitably produces evangelism. Paul teaches that evangelism and prayer are each ineffective without the other. To be more devoted to the activities of evangelism with little more than a token commitment to prayer will not bring the fruit God wants to give.

The protective wall that has protected America since our beginning as a Christian nation is coming down brick by brick. For approximately forty years we have been "sticking our finger in the eye of God" as we have progressively turned away from Him. We've taken prayer out of the schools and public arenas and have allowed over 40 million unborn babies to be murdered, just to name a couple. We have shown the opposite of what is written on our coins, "In God we trust."

As a result we suffer calamities and disasters, both natural and those caused by mankind, on a daily basis. As we look at biblical prophecy, there is not a single thing concerning the end times that is not evident today. The signs of nature (Matthew 24:7; Luke 21:11), signs of society (Matthew 24:12,37-39), spiritual signs (Matthew 24:5,9,11,14,24; 2 Thessalonians 2:3; 1 Timothy 4:1; Joel 2:28-32; Daniel 12:4,9), signs of technology (Daniel 12:4), as well as the signs of world politics and Israel, which are prolific throughout the Bible.

As we lift our eyes from our nation to our world, we are shocked to witness blatant persecution against Christians, even torture and death in many places. Will America be exempt? Christians are already considered the "dangerous, radical religious right" and ridiculed on TV and in movies and magazines, and it only intensifies with every passing year.

The AIDS virus is devastating much of Africa right now, and people in the West seem oblivious to the suffering. In fact more have died from AIDS than were killed in all the wars of the past century.

Russia is no longer our only nuclear enemy. Many rogue nations are arming themselves now. Where will it end? For an interesting viewpoint on Bible prophecy, I suggest reading the *Left Behind* series of novels. (Tim LaHaye and Jerry Jenkins, Wheaton, IL: Tyndale House Publishers).

As see the many judgments of God coming on us, we have no guarantee that life will continue much longer as it has in the past. God is giving us plenty of warning. As it was with Gomorrah, He is holding back His wrath until the harvest is gathered in.

Denominational leaders worldwide believe we are wrapping up the 6,000 years of man. Numbers have a significant meaning in Scripture. Three is always the number of unity. Six is the number of imperfection or of man. Seven is the perfect number, the number of completion. Eight is the number of eternity.

No one knows the day or the hour of the Lord's return, but Jesus told us to watch the blooming of the fig tree to know the season.

> "Now learn this parable from the fig tree: When its branch has already become tender and puts forth leaves, you know that summer is near. So you also, when you see all these things, know that it is near—at the doors! Assuredly, I say to you, this generation will by no means pass away till all these things take

> place. Heaven and earth will pass away, but My words will by no means pass away" (Matthew 24:32-35).

The fig tree represents Israel. After being dispersed throughout the world for thousands of years, Israel became a nation again in May of 1948. They regained Jerusalem as their capital in June of 1967 in the Six-Day War. A generation in Scripture is generally forty years. God wants us to be aware of the season by watching the fig tree, but He is clear that no one can predict the exact timetable.

> "But of that day and hour no one knows, not even the angels of heaven, but My Father only. But as the days of Noah were, so also will the coming of the Son of Man be. For as in the days before the flood, they were eating and drinking, marrying and giving in marriage, until the day that Noah entered the ark, and did not know until the flood came and took them all away, so also will the coming of the Son of Man be. Then two men will be in the field: one will be taken and the other left. Two women will be grinding at the mill: one will be taken and the other left. Watch therefore, for you do not know what hour your Lord is coming. But know this, that if the master of the house had known what hour the thief would come, he would have watched and not allowed his house to be broken into. Therefore you also be ready, for the Son of Man is coming at an hour you do not expect" (Matthew 24:36-44).

Once believers in Jesus Christ have been removed from the earth to attend the marriage feast of the Lamb, a seven-year period of tribulation begins on the earth. Our salvation is secured through Jesus Christ alone, but our works will be tested and our rewards determined. Believers face the judgment seat of Christ immediately upon our translation into heaven. This becomes the reward seat of Christ. This is only one of six judgments in the New Testament. If you'd like to read about the others, I will list the passages where they are found. The judgment of the Cross itself (Romans 8:34), the judgment of angels (1 Corinthians 6:3; 2 Peter 2:4), the judgment of the church (1 Corinthians 5:13), the Sheep and Goat Judgment (Matthew 25:32-46), and the Great White Throne Judgment (Revelation 20:11-15).

"For no other foundation can anyone lay than that which is laid, which is Jesus Christ. Now if anyone build on this foundation with gold, silver, precious stones, wood, hay straw, each one's work will become clear; for the Day will declare it, because it will be revealed by fire; and the fire will test each one's work, of what sort it is. If anyone's work which he has built on it endures, he will receive a reward. If anyone's work is burned, he will suffer loss; but he himself will be saved, yet so as through fire" (I Corinthians 3:11-15).

That period of time will close out with a great war in the Valley of Megiddo in Israel. Jesus will come from heaven and end it with a word. There will be no need for Him or the armies of heaven (us!) with Him to "fire a shot".

"Now I saw heaven opened, and behold, a white horse. And He who sat on him was called Faithful and True, and in righteousness He judges and makes war. His eyes were like a flame of fire, and on His head were many crowns. He had a name written that no one knew except Himself. He was clothed with a robe dipped in blood, and his name is called The Word of God. And the armies in heaven, clothed in fine linen, white and clean, followed Him on white horses. Now out of His mouth goes a sharp sword, that with it He should strike the nations. And He Himself will rule them with a rod of iron. He Himself treads the winepress of the fierceness and wrath of Almighty God. And He has on His robe and on His thigh a name written: KING OF KINGS AND LORD OF LORDS" (Revelation 19:11-16).

Very soon Jesus Christ will be ruling and reigning on earth as King of Kings and Lord of Lords for a thousand years, and we will be reigning with Him. Following that millennium, time as we know it will end. In Revelation 22, the last chapter in the Bible, the phrase "I am coming quickly" is repeated three times. "Come" is repeated four times. At the end of the previous chapter it is clear that "only those who are written in the Lamb's Book of Life" (Revelation 21:27b) will be allowed to enter heaven.

If you would like a "play by play" of what is yet to happen on the timeline of history, go to the book of Revelation and read all 22 chapters.

Many of us put various things before our primary relationship with our Bridegroom: money, houses, cars, clothes, TV and movies, entertainment, shopping, food, addictive substances, secular romance novels, magazines and books, sports, games, friends, vacations, fantasizing, illicit relationships ... you name it. Christians have a lot of addictions, and many are even considered acceptable in the church.

If we're not addicted to Jesus, we're addicted to something else. If your heart is not satisfied with Him, it will continually be longing after other things in an attempt to fill that void. Remember that *anything* you put ahead of your Bridegroom will dull your spiritual eyes, ears, heart, and spirit.

> "As the Father loved Me, I also have loved you; abide in My love. If you keep My commandments, you will abide in My love, just as I have kept My Father's commandments and abide in His love. These things I have spoken to you, that My joy may remain in you, and that your joy may be full" (John 15:9-11).

I encourage you to read that entire chapter in John for a reminder of what a passionate love relationship with Jesus entails. If I had to choose my favorite chapter in the Bible, this would be the one.

Until this most basic truth is fleshed out in our lives, we will have absolutely no impact on the lost world around us, whether it's our husbands and children within our own homes, our next door neighbors, or the lost masses in our nation and beyond to the world. I believe with all my heart that we are very close to the return of our Lord Jesus Christ, and that we will all be standing before Him very soon. Are you ready to meet Him face to face?

As we look at all of the incredible needs in our nation and the world today, sometimes we become catatonic, like a deer caught in the headlights of an oncoming car. We really don't believe in our heart of hearts that we can make a difference, so we choose to do nothing of any eternal consequence as a result. We need to ask God to give us fresh new eyes of faith and hope for the future, regardless of our age or stage in life.

Our eldest son, Trey, has had a strong desire to serve the Lord all of his life. This is a poem that he wrote when he was fourteen years old for his freshman Honors English class.

The Mission

Finish saying goodbye to family and friends,
You're a big kid now.
You're leaving home for good you know,
You've made your wedding vow.

You've picked the work that fits you best,
You've taken years of school.
You've worked really hard and passed the test,
And now your job's real cool.

As you leave the car and board the plane,
You feel kind of sad.
You're leaving behind so many things,
Especially your Mom and Dad.

Sitting with your wife on the plane,
You clutch her hand real tight.
You're not sure where the Lord will take you,
But you'll trust Him with all your might.

When you touch down in another country,
It feels really weird.
Being a missionary is that way sometimes,
That's the way it's geared.

Knowing where to get started,
Is kind of hard to learn.
But with the Lord on your side,
You'll know which way to turn.

Tabernacle Truth

The cry from God is always His desire that we return to Him. "'Return to Me,'" says the Lord of hosts, 'and I will return to you'" (Zechariah 1:3). This call is repeated in various ways throughout the Bible, a call to repentance and restoration of our love relationship with our Bridegroom. It starts with a heart of humility and obedience. This is personal revival. Once we have established (or reestablished) this primary relationship, it is His desire that we spread that passion to others.

"The harvest truly is plentiful, but the laborers are few. Therefore pray the Lord of the harvest to send out laborers into His harvest" (Matthew 9:37b, 38). What brings increase? In the sixth chapter of Acts the twelve disciples of Jesus said, "We will give ourselves continually to prayer and to the ministry of the word" (vs. 4). The result of that is given three verses later. "Then the word of God spread, and the number of the disciples multiplied greatly in Jerusalem" (vs. 7a). The priority of the apostles in the early church was to pray in the harvest and minister the word of God.

From the Old Testament to the New Testament, from Genesis to Revelation, we get the same message. What was the last thing Jesus said before He disappeared into the clouds as He ascended into heaven?

> "All authority has been given to Me in heaven and on earth. Go therefore and make disciples of all the nations, baptizing them in the name of the Father and of the Son and of the Holy Spirit, teaching them to observe all things that I have commanded you; and lo, I am with you always, even to the end of the age." (Matthew 28:18b-20)

This call was given to *all* of Christ's followers. If we know Jesus as Savior, we are included in this last and great commission. We are to start where we are. We are right now living in our "Jerusalem" and that is where we are to start. We can serve effectively in our own homes, influencing our spouses and discipling our children. "The hand that rocks the cradle rules the world," it is said. I am so grateful to the Lord that our children, though far from perfect, are walking with God, growing as disciples, and sharing their faith with others. But God doesn't want me to stop here. He wants me to *start* here!

Maybe God will never lead you farther afield geographically, but maybe He will. He is the only one who knows His full plan for your life. However, there isn't one of us who can't pray to the ends of the earth in an instant, any hour of the day or night. God doesn't care if you're nine or ninety-nine. You can do it. God has answered prayer in the past, He is answering prayer in the present, and He will continue to answer prayer in the future. Dramatic results come when God's people pray. As we pray, we go. *Go* is the first part of both *God* and *gospel*! God enables us to help change the world, one person at a time.

All of us who know Christ personally have a personal testimony. Nothing is more effective to draw someone to Jesus Christ than personal testimony. It catches the attention of the listener and is an opportunity for us to identify with the unbeliever and show how Christ has made the difference in our lives.

Many of us are guilty of "copping out" by thinking that all that is required of us is to live a good life in front of others. When was the last time *you* were asked what makes you different? It is clear throughout the Word of God that we are all to share through the spoken word as well as through good works and the example of our character. Paul admonishes us all in First Corinthians 3:5-17 to be watering, working, and warning. We are all part of the worldwide harvest, to pray, to give, and to go. Going does not necessarily mean leaving home and family, but it does mean making yourself available to serve wherever, whenever, and however He directs.

As appealing as the marketplace is for both men and women, many find only disappointment and emptiness if they choose to invest their lives solely in fleeting achievements. Our greatest satisfaction is found in Christ and sharing Him with others, whether from our home or our place of employment. No matter what our position or circumstance, we will find ultimate joy and happiness only in Jesus Christ. We will be effective only as we serve in the place and the manner God directs. No task is insignificant when God calls you to do it.

If you are restless where you are right now, it is probable that God is trying to get your attention for change. It may be a geographical change, a job change, or a new challenge that He will reveal as you begin to truly seek His will for your life. "If anyone *wills* to do His will, he shall know concerning the doctrine, whether it is from God" (John 7:17a, emphasis mine). "Work out your own salvation with fear and trembling; for it is God who works in you both to *will* and to do for His good pleasure" (Philippians 2:12b-13, emphasis mine).

Taking initiative and being bold is not natural for everyone. Perhaps you are not bold or able to speak well because you have not asked God for these qualities. The disciples prayed for boldness and God answered their prayer. "Grant to Your servants that with all boldness they may speak Your word" (Acts 4:29b). Not only are we to pray for others to be effective in evangelism, we are also to ask God to make us personally effective in seizing every opportunity He gives us to speak.

> For the grace of God that brings salvation has appeared to all men, teaching us that, denying ungodliness and worldly lusts, we should live soberly, righteously, and godly in the present age, looking for the blessed hope and glorious appearing of our great God and Savior Jesus Christ, who gave Himself for us, that He might redeem us from every lawless deed and purify for Himself His own special people, zealous for good works. *Speak these things*, exhort, and rebuke with all authority (Titus 2:11-15a, emphasis mine).

If you are waiting for a time when everything is convenient, forget it. That time will never come. Solomon said, "He who observes the wind will not sow, and he who regards the clouds will not reap" (Ecclesiastes 11:4). Isaiah said, "Blessed are you who sow beside all waters" (32:20a). Luke said, "Ask, and it will be given to you; seek, and you will find; knock, and it will be opened to you" (11:9). Paul said, "And let us not grow weary while doing good, for in due season we shall reap if we do not lose heart" (Galatians 6:9).

We are to keep on keeping on. Let's be seed-minded, not need-minded.

Points to Ponder and Pray

"The Lord was with him and let none of his words fall to the ground" (1 Samuel 3:19). What do you think this verse says about

Samuel's ability to speak for the Lord? Are you willing to step out in faith to become a spokesperson for God? Let your mess become your message!

> So shall My word be that goes forth from My mouth;
> It shall not return to Me void,
> But it shall accomplish what I please,
> And it shall prosper in the thing for which I sent it
> (Isaiah 55:11).

God promises to use every word that you speak for Him. Give your fears over to Him. Remember that fear is **F**alse **E**vidence **A**ppearing **R**eal. Fear will paralyze your potential, ruin your relationships, hinder your happiness, and sabotage your success. We would love to walk on the water, but we don't want to get out of the boat!

Are you ready to throw your hat in the ring for the main event? Are you ready to stop looking at the clouds and start praying for rain? Have you ever really asked Him to use you? Are you willing to let Him take you out of your comfort zone? What is your response to Him?

Chapter 21

Passing the Mantle

When we returned from Ireland in 1986, I came back a very different woman from the one I was nearly twelve years earlier. I had left the U.S. as a twenty-seven-year-old pioneer with my young husband on the adventure of a lifetime. I returned a thirty-nine-year-old mother of four, older and wiser after having been tested and tried through the fires in countless ways by my Lord, the Master Designer of what He wants me to become.

That summer, I spent some time in the mountains of Colorado at my parent's vacation home. During my visit, I was inextricably drawn to a series of summer meetings being held at a little Baptist church nearby. My mom graciously looked after the children so I could go.

In the first meeting, I was amazed to discover that a little gray-haired lady, ninety-seven years old, was the speaker! As Miss Bertha Smith stood up there and shared story after story about her life as a single missionary in China, her message throughout was:

<u>Not I, But Christ</u>

Lord, bend that proud and stiff-necked "I",
Help me to bow the neck and die,
Beholding Him on Calvary,
Who bowed His head for me.
Anonymous

I felt the hand of God on me, and His voice in my ear, in a powerful way. I spent much of that week on my knees in a little alcove of that church, often in tears. In a powerful Holy Spirit experience of revival, I gave my life afresh to my Creator and Lord, to use me in whatever way He saw fit. I felt more insignificant than I had at eighteen, twenty, twenty-eight, or thirty. Without His power at work in my life, I knew I was absolutely nothing and had no hope.

A couple of years ago I discovered a book called *Women of Awakenings.*[1] I scanned the table of contents, which included such great women of the faith as Deborah from the Old Testament, Priscilla of the New Testament, Susanna Wesley, and Ruth Graham. But I was stunned to see a chapter on none other than Miss Bertha Smith, the little old lady God brought into my life during that difficult transitional summer. The faithfulness of one woman can be powerful. She passed her mantle on to me two years before she went to be with her Savior. In the same way, I would like to pass it on to you today, if you are willing to accept it.

I want to offer you some challenges as you finish reading this book. Begin to think in terms of moving in concentric circles from yourself to the ends of the earth – remembering that nothing is too hard for God! First, I strongly encourage you to make a commitment today with two friends to meet weekly for an hour to pray together as a triplet for at least a year. (When your group grows to six, I'd encourage you to split into two groups. It gives you more time to pray for all of your concerns if you keep your numbers small.) At this time next year, you won't believe how much God has blessed you, your family, your church, and your influence on others as a result. Put God to the test.

When we came to Orlando in 1991, the Lord gave me a small group of friends to pray with for an hour a week, as He'd done the previous four years in California. That group has since grown and split to form several other groups.

Jesus said, "Again I say to you that if two of you agree on earth concerning anything that they ask, it will be done for them by My Father in heaven. For where two or three are gathered together in My name, I am there in the midst of them" (Matthew 18:19-20).

After our Mayor's Prayer Breakfast in Orlando in May 1996, a man came up to me and introduced himself as the pastor of the first church I ever did a Passionate Hearts conference for, in February 1995. My eyes brimmed with tears as he related how their entire church had changed as a result of the prayer triplets formed that weekend, and that their women's retreat this year almost tripled. The faithfulness of one woman, in this case his wife who organized the conference, was the conduit for change.

A few months after conducting a conference for a church in Sanford, Florida, I got an excited call from the woman who organized it. She was overjoyed as she recounted how their entire church had come into revival as a result of the women getting right with God and becoming serious about prayer. Bitterness and strife disappeared, relationships were healed, broken families came together, and 5:30 A.M. prayer meetings were held at the church daily. The faithfulness of one person can bring change.

In February 1996, one year into the ministry of Passionate Hearts, God woke me before dawn one morning. He impressed upon me that the next step was to challenge women to be catalysts to draw other women together from every church and denomination in their communities to a city-wide prayer gathering. Within forty-eight hours God confirmed that message with a call from a dear friend, Peg Yelverton, in North Carolina. She told me that God had awakened *her* and impressed her that she was to organize a conference in Wilmington, North Carolina. She was calling to ask if I could advise her on what that meant.

On April 4, 1997, Peg obediently brought to pass that call from God with a citywide fasting and prayer gathering called "Wake Up, Wilmington." It was a wonderful success, with Christian radio stations and many churches coming on board to help. God led Peg to do a forty-day fast in the fall of 1996 in preparation for this, which she repeated a year later as she organized a Passionate Hearts mother/daughter conference for her church in November 1997.

God has been growing Peg from strength to strength as a result of her obedience over the past few years. She is now teaching a Bible Study Fellowship group of about 400 women. The faithfulness of one woman can bring great change.

During the second week of my first forty-day fast in 1996, God led me to organize a Fasting and Prayer Gathering in Orlando to unite women of all denominations and churches to come together to fast and pray for our nation.[2] We had about 100 women. In May 1997, I spoke at a women's prayer breakfast with Edith Schaeffer on the National Day of Prayer in Tampa, Florida, where about 1,800 women were in attendance.

Whether it's 100 or 2,000, we are to move ahead by faith. The numbers are up to Him. The obedience is up to us.

If you'd like to organize something with a stronger punch, consider a weekend for women at your church or a residential retreat. My partner, Nancy Wilson, or I would be delighted to come to lead a conference for you. If you would like details on how to do this, please check the appendix for details.

There has never been a prayer-less revival. Prayer is always the forerunner of revival. You simply can't have an extraordinary outpouring of the Spirit without an extraordinary outpouring of prayer. Prayer is the key that unlocks the power of God in revival. To put it more precisely, "prayer is the root, revival is the fruit." Prayer must be our first recourse, not our last resort.

Lift up your eyes from your church and take the challenge to your city. It bears repeating that in Esther 4:14, Mordecai told his niece that if she remained silent, God would find someone else, but he believed she had been placed there for a purpose: *"for such a time as this."* In the same way, you are right now in the right place at the right time, and He is giving you the opportunity and the privilege of being used. God will give you success.

My heart's desire is to see prayer triplets in every church, school, workplace, and neighborhood in this nation and around the world, and that men, women, and young people would begin to reach out to their neighbors and friends who don't know Christ. As people of all ages take up the standard and begin to walk in intimacy with God, we will begin to see revival in our hearts, our families, neighborhoods, churches, cities, and eventually in our nation and the world. I'm praying that as I tell you of some of my dreams, God will ignite a dream in your heart.

Tabernacle Truth

During the period of history when God lived among His people in the wilderness Tabernacle, the high priest would enter the Holy of Holies once a year to atone for the sins of the people.The blood of the animals that were slain at the altar of sacrifice would be sprinkled on the mercy seat, which covered the Ark of the Covenant.

Once Jesus Christ, our sacrificial Lamb, shed His blood *once for all* at the cross of Calvary, there is no longer a need for sacrificial animals. As our great High Priest, He has paid the ultimate price to secure our salvation and freedom from the bondage of sin. *God anoints what the blood has covered!*

As believer-priests, we also have the privilege of coming before God on behalf of the people. "'The word is near you, in your mouth and in your heart' (that is, the word of faith which we preach): that if you confess with your mouth the Lord Jesus and believe in your heart that God has raised Him from the dead, you will be saved. For with the heart one believes unto righteousness, and with the mouth confession is made unto salvation" (Romans 10:8-10). We cannot receive forgiveness for them, but we can be a travel advisory on their journey to show them the way to the Altar of Sacrifice and how to proceed on into the Holy of Holies.

The relationship between God and man is no longer limited to laws written on tablets of stone. Scripture states, "I will put My laws into their hearts and in their minds I will write them" (Hebrews 10:16). Continued intimacy with God leads to a life filled with the fruit of the indwelling Holy Spirit. Abundant spiritual fruit in our lives is the outward manifestation of this inner transformation. It is the ability to glorify God in every earthly endeavor.

"So the Lord spoke to Moses face to face, as a man speaks to his friend (Exodus 33:11a). What an awesome privilege! In the same way, our relationship with our heavenly Father through the Holy Spirit must be one of intimate closeness, yet of respect, as a son who is privileged to call his father "Daddy." This relationship should be more real and inspiring than any other in our life. Such intimacy leaves everything open and laid bare in His presence.

God's heart-cry for intimacy with man has been echoing down through the ages. The Father beckoned His people in the Sinai wilderness with this message. Jesus sent His Holy Spirit to live within us to accomplish greater intimacy with Himself in preparation for us to be eternally one with the Father. The Holy Spirit is urging us, the bride, to join with Him in praying for Jesus' return.

"And the Spirit and the bride say, "Come!" And let him who hears say, "Come!" And let him who thirsts come. Whoever desires, let him take the water of life freely. Surely I am coming quickly" (Revelation 22:17, 20b).

A bride calling her bridegroom — the Bridegroom wooing his long-awaited mate — what could be more tender and intimate? Jesus promised that as the Bridegroom, *He will return* to claim His bride. We are that bride and are preparing to be presented to Him on our wedding day.

Will His call continue indefinitely? No. The moment will soon be upon us when God's plea for intimacy with man will cease. He will return suddenly. "Remember therefore how you have received and heard; hold fast and repent. Therefore if you will not watch, I will come upon you as a thief, and you will not know what hour I will come upon you" (Revelation 3:3). Every other promise God made to His people through the centuries He has fulfilled. He will consummate this one also.

Are we prepared to meet Him? How clean are our garments? "Christ also loved the church and gave Himself for her, that He might sanctify and cleanse her with the washing of water by the word, that He might present her to Himself a glorious church, not having spot or wrinkle or any such thing, but that she should be holy and without blemish" (25b-27).

A marriage celebration awaits us! "Let us be glad and rejoice and give Him glory, for the marriage of the Lamb has come, and His wife has made herself ready. And to her it was granted to be arrayed in fine linen, clean and bright, for the fine linen is the righteous acts of the saints (Revelation 19:7-8).

As you look back at what you have learned about the Tabernacle, take a sheet of paper and a pen. Draw a straight line from the gate at the east end to the mercy seat at the west, and another line from the lamp stand at the south to the table at the north. What do you see? The cross of Jesus Christ! Is it any wonder that everything in the Tabernacle is a picture of Him? Christ is the Door. He is both the High Priest and the Sacrifice. Christ is the Bronze Laver, the Golden Lampstand, the Bread of the Presence, the Altar of Incense, the Veil, the Ark, and the Mercy Seat. Yes, Christ Jesus is the true Tabernacle.

I can't show you the actual Old Testament Tabernacle, but I can do one better. If you've received Christ as your Savior, then look in the mirror. You are that temple. That body you might like to trade in for a newer version is sacred. Psalm 139 says that we are "fearfully and wonderfully made" (v. 14). He is God, and He chooses to live in you and me. This is the way He dwells among the people of this world. How deeply will you allow God to draw you into His dwelling place is a choice only you can make.

Our third son, Joshua, came into our master bedroom one night just after his sixteenth birthday and handed me a poem. "Mom," he said, "the Lord impressed me to write this about how I feel about Him." As I read the poem and looked up at my fair-haired son, the son God had saved from the jaws of a vicious dog at the age of three, I realized that he was fast becoming a man. My eyes filled with tears as I wished that everyone on earth could experience the simplicity of a love relationship like this with their heavenly Father. This is my prayer for you.

This is the poem God gave to my son.

With You

Josh,
When you were born,
I loved you.
When you accepted Me as your Lord and Savior,
I rejoiced with the angels in heaven.
At night when you would read your Bible and pray,
I was overwhelmed with joy
Because I got to spend time with you.
When you were sleeping,
I would run My fingers through your hair
And whisper words of love in your ear.
When you walked outside,
I would embrace you with the warmth of the sun
And caress your face with the cool breeze.
If you only knew how much I love you!
I'm earnestly awaiting the next time
I can spend some time with you.
Jesus

Points to Ponder and Pray

"Therefore, brethren, having boldness to enter the Holiest by the blood of Jesus, by a new and living way which He consecrated for us, through the veil, that is, His flesh, and having a High Priest over the house of God, let us draw near with a true heart in full assurance of faith, having our hearts sprinkled from an evil conscience and our bodies washed with pure water. Let us hold fast the confession of our hope without wavering, for He who promised is faithful. And let us consider one another in order to stir up love and good works, not forsaking the assembling of ourselves together, as is the manner of some, but exhorting one another, and so much the more as you see the Day approaching" (Hebrews 10:19-25).

We enter God's presence the same way we are saved, by confession. We are not examining our own faithfulness – we are confessing God's faithfulness. We are confessing and testifying to the cleansing power of the blood of Jesus.

Has He pierced the deepest intents of your heart so that you really yearn to know Him? Are you willing to count the cost of intimacy with Him? Yes, it is costly. It requires commitment, effort, sacrifice, and time, but the rewards are immeasurable. Do you really want to know Him, simply for the sake of knowing Him? Just for the privilege of kneeling in His awesome presence? Then you may enter the Holy of Holies. Right here. Right now.

Enter boldly. Enter as a true son or daughter of the household of faith, nothing wavering. *He who promised is faithful.*

Appendix

Courtship: The Answer to a Successful Marriage

While going through the checkout line at the grocery store, a number of magazines try to explain the way to pursue a successful marriage. When in-fact, all their helpful information doesn't seem to help much. Many people are distressed over the record-high rates of divorce, illegitimacy, teenage pregnancy, marital infidelity, and premarital promiscuity. On some issues, there is an emerging consensus that something is drastically wrong. There was a time when divorces used to barely exist. Now, it's nearly abnormal to have parents that are still together. People talk about doing something to slow the rate of divorce, when very little attention is paid to what leads to marital success. Still we refuse to attend to the ways practiced in the past. There is, of course, good reason for this neglect. The very terms- "wooing," "courting," "suitors" are seen as ancient; and if the words barely exist, it is because the described phenomena have all but disappeared. It is my view, despite arguments to the contrary, that courtship is a way of working towards marriage that is, and has been, an extremely successful way to prepare for marriage.

Courtship is beneficial to future marriages for a number of reasons. First, it encourages an open relationship whereas dating often isolates a couple from other vital relationships. These differences are explained in an article from Harper's Magazine named "A Date with the Family" written by Jim and Anne Ryun: "Dating means waving goodbye at the door and saying, "Be home by midnight," whereas courtship includes time spent with the entire family. In our home, a young man interested in Heather or our youngest daughter, Catherine, is apt to find himself playing basketball with our twin sons, Ned and Drew, or helping out in the kitchen after dinner." Courtship not only opens up communication with the family but also with other friends. Therefore, courtship not only benefits the couple's relationship but the relationships they have with others.

Dating in many cases distracts the young couple from their responsibility to prepare for the future. A dating relationship lacks the tools to adequately prepare them for marriage. Instead of equipping themselves with character, education, and experience necessary to succeed in life, many allow themselves to be consumed by the present needs that dating emphasizes. Maintaining a relationship takes a lot of time and energy. Couples spend countless hours talking, writing, thinking, and often worrying about their relationship. The energy they exert just ends up stealing away from other more useful pursuits. Dating may help people practice being good boyfriends and girlfriends, but what are these skills worth? Courtship doesn't usually teach people how to be the perfect boyfriend or girlfriend, but it does teach some effective ways of dealing with relational problems that might occur during marriage.

Although most dating relationships don't head toward marriage, people who sincerely want to find out if someone is a potential partner should understand that dating may actually hinder that process. Joshua Harris explains this idea in his book, *I Kissed Dating Goodbye,* "Dating creates an artificial environment that doesn't demand that a person accurately portray his or her positive and negative characteristics. On a date, a person can charm his or her way into a date's heart. He drives a nice car and pays for everything. She looks beautiful, but who cares? Being fun on a date doesn't say much about a date's character or ability to be a good husband or wife." This is not to say that a marriage doesn't require a love relationship.

After marriage, dating is one of the main ways of keeping a deeper love relationship going, but people seeking marriage just in the confines of a dating relationship may miss the more important experiences needed for marriage. People weighing the possibility of marriage need to make sure they don't just interact within the fun, romantic settings of dating. Their priority shouldn't be to get away from real life. Courtship enables a couple to watch each other serving or working while seeing how each interacts with people who know them best. It is often helpful to see how the person reacts when things go wrong. Again, dating fails to create a real life environment that will help a marriage develop. Courtship, on the other hand, helps prepare couples to experience the kind of things that are helpful once they are married.

Can courtship make a comeback in today's society? It's doubtful since it's based on the fact that it was a way to prepare for marriage that our Grandparents used. Young people today tend to shy away from the things of the past. I believe courtship is part of the solution to lowering the rates of divorce, illegitimacy, teenage pregnancy, marital infidelity, and premarital promiscuity. First, it would require men to start respecting women, and not acting like someone who is just "looking to score." This might also require women to guard their purity. If women denied men the easy satisfaction of "free" sex, and guarded their purity for their husband, it might motivate men to want to be that kind of man; turning lust into love. Courtship may seem to be a quaint and somewhat ineffective way of working towards marriage, but by looking at the facts, it is evident that between courtship and dating it would be foolish to choose the latter.

Joshua Killingsworth
College Freshman
December 2, 2000

Emotional Abstinence: Adopting God's Plan as my Own

I remember myself as a dejected tenth grader sitting on the curb outside Taco Bell after a Friday night football game, tears wetting my cheeks and a vacant look in my eyes. It was at this time in my life that I felt that I was truly in love, even though my pursuits of relational intimacy were lying at my feet in shreds.

I wish I had realized in that sad moment that any romantic pursuits during my high school career would ultimately end in frustration and emotional upheaval. It wasn't until recently, some time after another significant heartbreak, that I realized just how imperative emotional abstinence is during these potentially volatile teen years. I share this with you out of a heavy burden that God has given me to help other young adults escape the vice of premature emotional codependence on the opposite sex. In Proverbs 4:23, Solomon warns his son to "Keep your heart with all diligence, for out of it spring the issues of life." Allow me to share with you some of the peripheral issues that surround this concept coined "emotional abstinence."

I plan on having an incredible marriage relationship in the future with a woman that God has handpicked for me to spend the rest of my life with. It would be incredibly foolish for me to do anything at this point in my life that might harm that relationship. What am I referring to? Finding someone of the opposite sex who will pacify my desire for relational intimacy during high school. It is extraordinarily difficult for teenagers, like myself, to maintain a long-term perspective as it pertains to our future spouse. In this light, relationships between teenagers – especially high school students – begin to appear genuinely superficial. When you begin the process of getting to know someone on an intimate level, you set into motion an irreversible chain of events that God intended to result in marriage. This process also operates in the physical aspect of an exclusive relationship with someone of the opposite sex. When you begin experiencing physical intimacy, God intended those affections to lead directly to sex. I know that anyone would concede how difficult it is to bridle physical intimacy. It's virtually impossible, and God meant it to be that way. If a couple gets involved physically, they are defrauding each other and stifling God's design, because they're not in a position to enjoy God's gift of sex. The same is unequivocally true of emotional intimacy. If a couple starts getting emotionally involved during high school, they defraud each other and stifle God's perfect plan for their lives because they're not at a state in life when they can enjoy marriage, which is the perfect context for emotional-codependence.

This realization was a hard one, because it runs counter to the expectations society has placed on me. According to the majority of society, it's perfectly normal and healthy to date someone for a few weeks/months before it inevitably dissolves and you start the process over again (long-term relationships are even more damaging, in my estimation). Basically, you're pretending to be married, which means a breakup has the emotional ramifications of divorce. The kind of pattern that develops is a string of short-term relationships with the potential to undermine your future marriage to someone. Emotional abstinence is the key to experiencing God's best.

I challenge you to follow my example and re-examine your view of relationships during this period of preparation for marriage. Let God make Himself real to you as you trust Him solely for the emotional sustenance that only He can provide. Will you join me?

Striving to keep the faith,

Jason Killingsworth
High School Senior
August 19, 1996

Emotional Abstinence
Carriers of the Light

Earlier this month, I attended the Southland Conference at Camp Kulaqua. Over the course of five days, I prayed that the Lord would intensify His sanctification in my life. It was a prayer decisively answered.

I didn't come to camp under the wrong pretense. In fact, I truly intended to focus on sanctification. But, alas, as I've learned so many times, infatuation hits when you're not looking for it. Her name was Katy, and I seemed to have a special connection with her, one that I can only refer to as supernatural. We became close quickly, much too quickly in fact, and soon I found myself knee-deep in a shamefully low state. It was at that second that the Lord spoke.

I remember it well. My best friend, Jason, and I were conversing about a topic which now escapes me (not surprisingly since it must have been 2 a.m.). As we were talking, I suddenly felt crushed spiritually — broken, in fact — and I simply said, "this dating thing is not for me." It was at that moment that I realized how useless I sounded. I was full of self-pity and remorse over my situation. Had the Lord not acted then, the enemy might have been able to build a stronghold in my life. Thankfully, Satan failed.

What is "Emotional Abstinence"?

As revealed to me, emotional abstinence is the act of keeping pure emotionally as well as physically, not giving yourself emotionally to someone until you are ready to marry that person. The purpose of emotional abstinence is to continue the work of being made increasingly holy and pure. Purity is absolutely vital to an effective witness and instrumental in a close personal relationship with our Savior.

Why be emotionally abstinent?

I think we'd all agree that one of the chief pursuits in life is security. The world finds security in material possessions, in personal ability, and in worldly success. As defenders of the truth, we find our security in the *personification* of truth, Jesus Christ. To experience lasting security we must have trust and, if our security is found in God, we must trust Him fully.

Trust in God is a difficult matter for the complacent and spiritually retired. Why trust in anything other than yourself if nothing distresses you? Therefore, those called to His purpose should expect to find distress during the building of this trust. The only cure for this distress is abandonment, 100% trust in God's will and total devotion to His purpose. The unfortunate fact is that many Christians fail to reach that point of spiritual maturity. They allow other things to stand in the way of developing a total trust, a sound security. For many Christians, what stands in the way is a co-dependent relationship. Not with God, but with one of His children.

You see, I form this opinion from my own failures. There is someone out there whom God has handpicked for me. Therefore, why waste time on superficial, month-long relationships. Not to say that a lengthy dating relationship is somehow justified. Quite the opposite is true. I've seen the most spiritual damage sustained by couples who have been together for so long that a strong interdependence forms.

This dependence is the core of the problem. It makes us comfortable. It whispers that we can rely on God totally as well as place a total trust in our girlfriend/boyfriend. An emotional crutch is formed, and we don't have to lean on God fully. However, when that relationship ends, the crutch is gone, and we are left on the ground wondering where our support is. At this point, repentance is key. Brokenness must be achieved and a new composition must overtake us. Not by our hand, but by Jesus Christ's.

So, this leads to my focus, which is God's design. While at camp, our guest speaker kept speaking on shattering God's design for our lives, and how it brings about damage. It is my firm commitment and utmost prompting that emotional abstinence is God's design! If it isn't, why is our walk inevitably damaged at the falling of our emotional crutch? The thing that should concern us most is not only the damage to us, but to our future marriage. That's the tragedy! The Lord has planned a wonderful and fulfilling marriage, a marriage that not only blesses our spouse, our children, and ourselves, but also those around us! What reasons are there to put that blessing in jeopardy, especially in high school? I sure can't think of any.

It has come to my attention that there is a certain rationale that is widely regarded by teens, one that I myself bought into, that I must discuss. It is the reasoning that dating in teenage years is beneficial in that it prepares you for marriage by learning how to have mature relationships. This reasoning is faulty on two counts. First, I would have to agree that they are correct in saying that dating now prepares them for marriage – the *worldly* concept of marriage, that is. It is all too true, this frivolous attaching and breaking up does prepare them for the concept of the first marriage as some kind of warm-up, one that is expected to fail. Secondly, high school dating can hardly be described as mature. This is the same dating pattern that leads many to deep physical involvement as well as a certain measure of emotional scarring. This is the same dating pattern that I have seen lead countless sheep astray. This is the same dating pattern that has irreparably damaged the self-concept of countless teenagers. With these results, we can ascertain only one reason. We aren't looking for mature relationships; we're looking for maturity through relationships. Maturing of Christians is the job of our Lord.

My focus this year is on raising the standard, on starting to run the race again, on using this blessed time in our lives to please the Creator of the Universe. I hope and pray that the fire, which engulfs me, will engulf you as well. Allow the Spirit to work in you. Embrace sanctification; let these words cut you to the heart. I love you all, I will be praying for you and your future spouse. I will be praying for the Lord's work to lead you to him without reservation and without a personal agenda. Grace and Peace to you all.

In His Awesome Power — Your Brother,

James C. Kessler
High School Senior
August 19, 1996

The Veil

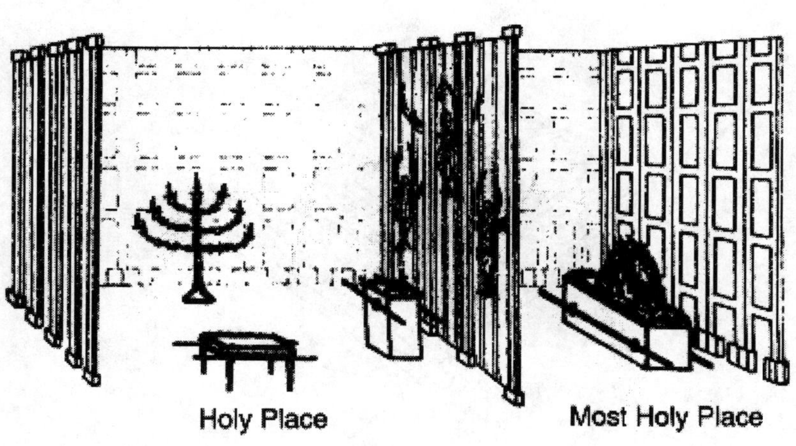

The Plan

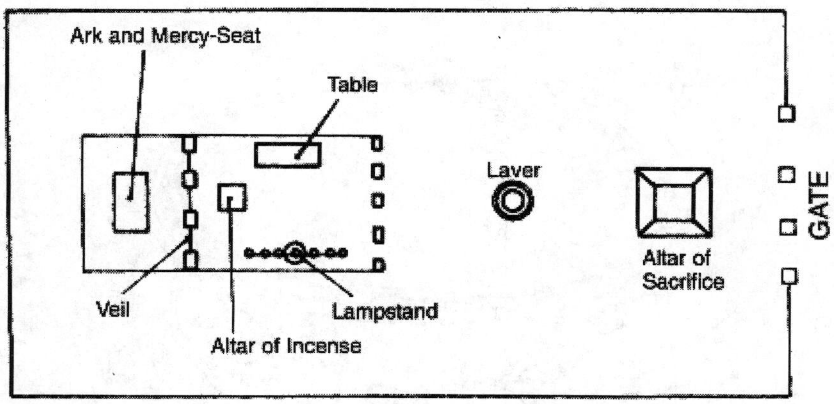

The Brazen Altar

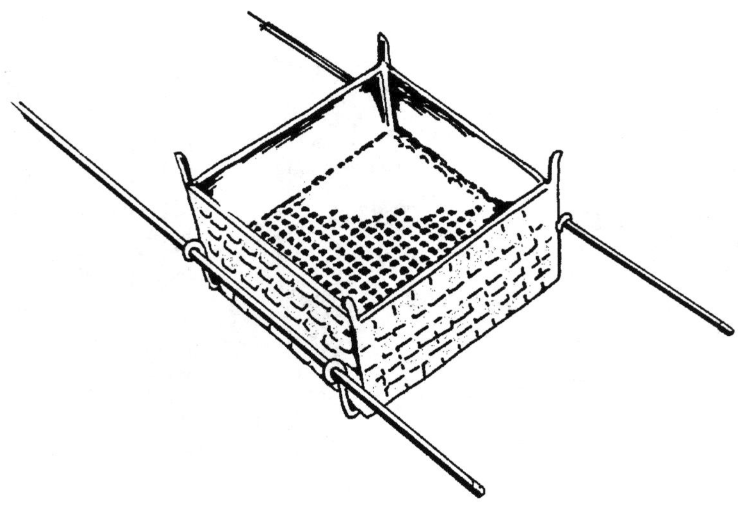

The Brass Washing Laver

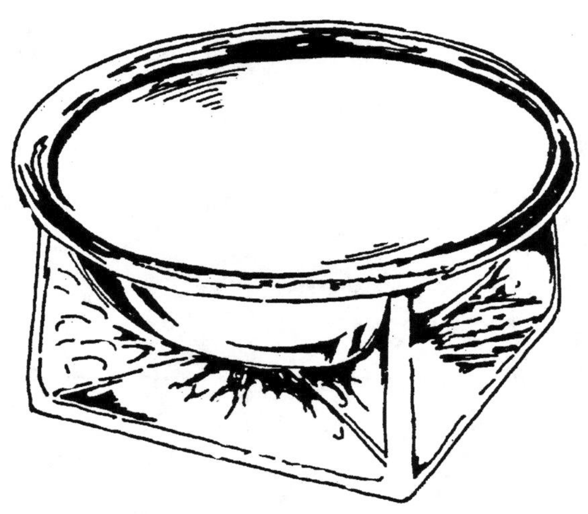

The Golden Lamp Stand

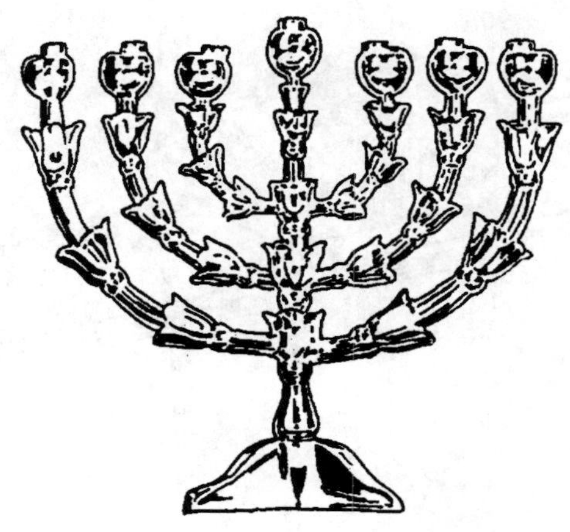

The Table of Shewbread

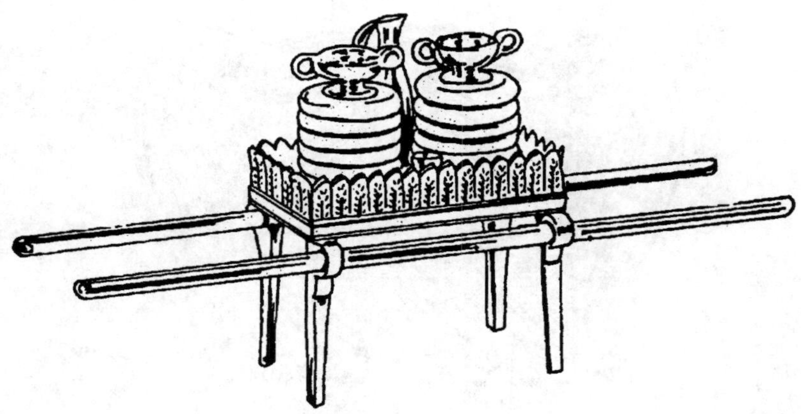

The Golden Altar of Incense

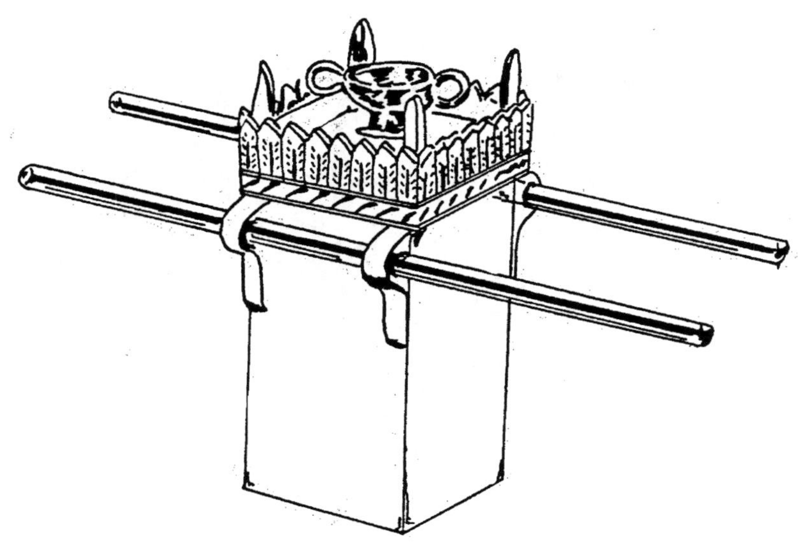

The Ark of the Covenant
and the Mercy Seat with Cherubim on Top

Steen Family Album

1950

1965

1968

1969

1970

1993

2001

Killingsworth Family Album

1970

1974

1975

1980

1985

1986

1988

1990

1993

1994

1995

1996

1997

1999

2001

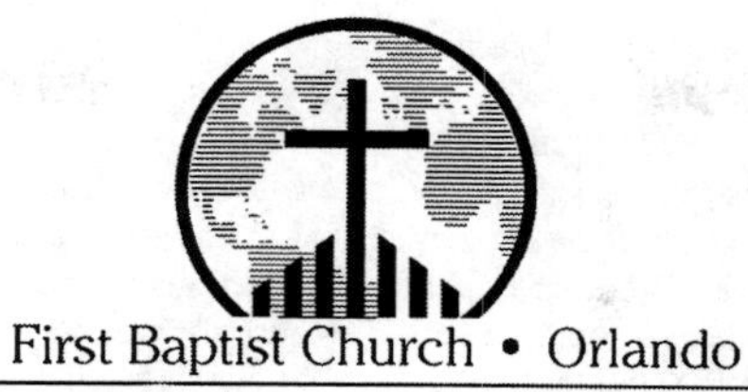

First Baptist Church • Orlando

May 22, 2001

Dear Brother Pastor,

I wish I could sit down with you and talk about the dreams you have for your church. I AM able to get in touch with you about the Passionate Hearts Conference for women. Laurie Killingsworth leads these special times for women and has done 35 conferences over the last five years for women's groups in churches from Seattle WA, So. California, to ours here in Central Florida. The results from Laurie's Conferences, just as for the many functions at which she's spoken here at First Baptist, have been uniformly God honoring.

Laurie and her husband, Tip, have faithfully served in our church for the past ten years and I've watched their five children grow up to love and serve the Lord so I know their walk matches their talk. Laurie and Tip have recently gone to help our newest "daughter church", The Fellowship of Orlando, out near Lake Nona.

I have heard that as Laurie gives her Women of Power, Women of Purity and Women of Prayer messages in these conferences, God's Spirit power is released as your women are drawn to intimacy with God. Laurie has prayed unceasingly for me over the years she and Tip have been in our church!

Please phone her at 434-546-0444 and chat with her about how she can be a help in what you want to see happen in the spiritual life of your women and your church. Her email address is laurie@passionatehearts.org if you would like to email her.

Thanks for giving me this chance to introduce Laurie to you and God bless as you serve the Lord.

In Christ,

Jim Henry

Jim Henry
Sr. Pastor
First Baptist Church/Orlando

THE CAMPUS MINISTRY

CAMPUS CRUSADE FOR CHRIST

Aaron Read
Director
5119 N.W. 24th Drive
Gainesville, FL 32605
Phone: (352) 376-6982
Fax: (352) 377-7932
E-Mail:
74152.1661@compuserve.com

Dear Campus Director,

I am writing to you in regards to some exciting things that we are experiencing in our movement at the University of Florida. The size of our movement has almost tripled in less than a year, students are sharing their faith with friends and family members, prayer is no longer another activity during the week, student ownership is at an all time high....what is going on? We believe that the Lord is answering prayers because things haven't always been this way.

Aaron and I have been on staff together at UF for 7 years. I came from a campus where ministry was fairly easy. Nothing was easy about UF. Aaron and I began praying more intensely asking the Lord to do something...anything. Over the years we have had 3 consistent requests: revival in the lives of believers, lost men and women coming to Christ, and for UF to be a sending ground for laborers. There were periods of discouragement for me as I wandered if the Lord even heard us at all. The Lord confirmed that we were in the right place and He continued giving us vision for what He could do on our campus.

Almost three years ago, Aaron fasted for 40 days. He went before the Lord on behalf of the future of our campus. One of Aaron's biggest concerns was the freshman class. We have all heard Roger Hershey talk about the importance of reaching the freshman if we are going to reach the campus. Aaron spent a lot of his time praying for the incoming freshman. That fall we saw more freshman get involved and STAY involved than ever before. Aaron completed a second 40 day fast in the fall as some of our staff and students joined him in various ways to pray for our campus. We strongly believe that the Lord is choosing to honor these requests. Prayer has made the difference.

With the lack of women staff on our campus, we were committed to having mini-retreats for the women to pull together to build unity in our movement this year. In January, Laurie Killingsworth came to minister to our women in a special way. I knew that she would be focusing on purity, power and prayer but I can't put into words the impact that she had that weekend. At the end of her first talk almost every girl in the room had something to confess publicly and asked for prayer. My heart was heavy from some of the things shared yet rejoiced because of the bonds that were released that night. Relationships were restored between friends and family, commitments were made to the Lord, and a fresh sense of pursuing the Him was on everyone's heart.

In the midst of such a hectic campus schedule, I would like to challenge you to look at the calendar NOW to schedule a retreat with Laurie. Even though I don't know what the remaining fruit will be from this weekend, I already can sense a more genuine spirit among our women and a hunger for God. I believe that God used Laurie to help give our women a vision for their walk with the Lord and living a dynamic life ministering for Him.

Sincerely,

Melody Read

Counseling Centers
Individual / Group Therapy
Employee Assistance Programs
Physician Practice Management
Management & Consulting Services

October 24, 2001

Mrs. Laurie Killingsworth
Passionate Hearts
Orlando, Florida

Subject: Conference at NorthRidge Church, Haines City, October 19,20, 2001

Dear Laurie,

On behalf of the women of our church, I would like to thank you for providing a lasting spiritual experience for our women. The timing of the two-day conference was perfect in that we are undergoing intense spiritual renewal in our church. The event allowed our women and opportunity to share their experiences as well as learn from your teaching.

I was encouraged to know that 70 % of our women have committed to having prayer triplets as an on-going prayer accountability. It was also exciting to know that 39% prayed for a fullness of the Holy Spirit in their Christian walk.

Thank you also for selecting the excellent books for your book table. As we do not have an active church library, it was great to seek the women choosing books that will feed them spiritually.

As you can see, we were pleased with the outcome of the event. I would welcome the opportunity to provide a reference to you for other groups who might be considering a similar event. I am enclosing a copy of the conference evaluation for your review.

Please give our love to Tip. We appreciated his music and service.

In friendship,

Bettye

M. Elizabeth West, Ed.D.
Event Coordinator

A Company of Bettye West & Associates, Inc.
Admiral's Inn, Suite 5013 • 5665 Cypress Gardens Blvd. • Winter Haven, Florida 33884 • (941) 325-8373 • Fax (941) 318-9170

STUDENT OPT-OUT NOTICE

To the ______________________________ School District.

Dear Sir or Madam:

1. Upon your receipt of this document, you are placed on legal notice that I(we), the undersigned parent(s), have elected to invoke my(our) parental rights as guaranteed by the U.S. Constitution, see, e.g., Troxel v. Granville, 530 U.S. 57, 66 (2000), and federal statute. See 20 U.S.C. § 1232h.

2. I hereby request that you not instruct my child about human sexuality without first providing me, on an incident-by-incident basis, at least 5 days prior notice, and obtaining my written permission after allowing me the opportunity to review your materials/lesson plan.

3. I hereby request that you specifically refrain from addressing issues of homosexuality, bisexuality, lesbianism, transvestitism, transsexuality, sado-masochism, pedophilia, bestiality or other alternatives to monogamous heterosexual sex within marriage to my child in any manner or form that would convey the message to my child that such orientations/behaviors are immutable, unchangeable, natural, normal, or harmless.

4. This request extends to any legitimization or normalization of these sexual orientations/behaviors no matter how your program or approach is defined, including but not limited to any instruction, materials or conversation related to "diversity," "tolerance," "multiculturalism," "gender studies," "family life," "safe schools," "hate crimes," "AIDS education," or the like.

5. This request extends to all school system employees and agents in any setting, on or off campus, in which my child(ren) is/are in the care of the school.

6. Any instruction that suggests that homosexuality is normal or acceptable is antithetical to my religious beliefs and/or my moral beliefs. Such instruction would therefore be a direct govern-mental intrusion on my rights and duties as a parent. I consider it the duty of the school to protect my child(ren) from any such activities.

7. I will regard the failure to notify me(us) of any of the aforementioned instruction and/or programs as an infringement of my(our) Procedural Due Process rights as guaranteed by the Fourteenth Amendment. See: Santosky v. Kramer, 455 U.S. 745, 753-760 (1982).
8. This document shall supersede any previously signed permission forms you may have on file.

The child(ren) to which this opt-out notice applies is/are:

_________________________ _________________________

_________________________ _________________________

Signed,

_________________________ ________

Parent or Legal Guardian Date

_________________________ ________

Parent or Legal Guardian Date

Booking and Ordering Information

To book a Passionate Hearts conference or retreat for your church, contact us at:

Passionate Hearts
P.O. Box 4784
Lynchburg, VA 24502-0784

laurie@passionatehearts.org
www.passionatehearts.org

Ordering Information for "One Passionate Heart" or the Passionate Hearts notebook:

1-5 copies:	$11.95 each
6-10 copies:	$10.95 each
Over 10 copies:	$ 9.95 each

Shipping and Handling: $2 per book
Check or money order payable to: *Passionate Hearts*

1) Lewis and Betty Drummond, Kregel Publications, Grand Rapids, MI, 1997.

2) An informative booklet "Preparing for the Coming Revival – How to Lead a Successful Fasting & Prayer Gathering", written by Dr. Bill Bright, is available from Campus Crusade for Christ, (407) 826-2000.